The Tree of Gernika · Gernikako arbola

The Bidart Family Collection, No. 1

THE TREE OF GERNIKA
GERNIKAKO ARBOLA
COMPLETE POEMS · BERTSOAK

JOXE MARI IPARRAGIRRE

TRANSLATION & NOTES · ITZULPENAK & OHARRAK
XABIER IRUJO & DAVID ROMTVEDT

FOREWORD · HITZAURRE
DAVID ROMTVEDT

CENTER FOR BASQUE STUDIES
UNIVERSITY OF NEVADA, RENO
2020

This book has been possible thanks to the Bidart family's commitment to Basque studies.

The Bidart Family Collection, No. 1

Series Editor: Xabier Irujo

Center for Basque Studies

University of Nevada, Reno

Reno, Nevada 89557

http://basque.unr.edu

Library of Congress Cataloguing-in-Publication Data

Names: Iparragirre, Joxe Mari, 1820-1881, author. | Irujo
    Ametzaga, Xabier, translator, editor. | Romtvedt, David, translator,
    editor, writer of foreword. | Iparragirre, Joxe Mari,
    1820-1881. Poems. | Iparragirre, Joxe Mari, 1820-1881.
    Poems. English.
Title: Gernikako arbola : bertsoak = The tree of Gernika : complete poems /
    by Joxe Mari Iparragirre ; translation & notes - Itzulpenak & Oharrak by
    Xabier Irujo & David Romtvedt ; foreword Hitzaurre by David Romtvedt.
Other titles: Tree of Gernika | Gernikako arbola.
Description: Reno : Center for Basque Studies, University of Nevada, Reno,
    2020. | Series: The Bidart Family collection ; no. 1 | Poems in Basque
    with parallel English translation.
Identifiers: LCCN 2020013063 | ISBN 9781949805260 (hardcover) |
    ISBN 9781949805239 (paperback)
Subjects: LCSH: Iparragirre, Joxe Mari,
    1820-1881--Translations into English. | LCGFT: Poetry.
Classification: LCC PH5339.I6 A2 2020 | DDC 899/.921--dc23
LC record available at https://lccn.loc.gov/2020013063

Contents

Foreword

The Basque poet, balladeer, guitarist, actor, former monarchist turned revolutionary seeker of freedom, Joxe Mari Iparragirre, was born on August 12, 1820 in Urretxu, Gipuzkoa, Euskal Herria, Earth, the Universe. His parents, after moving the family to Madrid when Joxe Mari was thirteen, enrolled their son in a Jesuit academy hoping he would enter the priesthood. But not long after the boy began his studies, the Carlist Wars—civil wars fought through the nineteenth century over succession to the Spanish crown—started, and Joxe Mari ran away from school and home. He found his way back to the Basque Country where, at age fourteen, he joined the army in support of Carlos, the Bourbon pretender who promised that if he were king the traditional Basque rights of autonomy—the foruak—would be maintained. Asked years later about his rash decision to go to war at fourteen, Joxe Mari said, "I had no opinion beyond love of my countrymen."

On the move with the Carlist army, the teenager carried both rifle and guitar. In his spare time, he practiced not marksmanship, but music, playing the guitar to accompany his newly composed songs and poems. After being injured twice in battle, he was one of the young men selected from the four southern Basque provinces to serve in the Royal Honor Guard to surely-soon-to-be King Carlos. And there he remained until the 1839 signing of the Bergarako Besarkada—the Embrace of Bergara. This treaty marked the defeat of

Carlos and the official end of the first Carlist Wars. It was the beginning of the end for Basque freedom.

Joxe Mari, now nineteen, refused to accept the embrace and so, like many other Basques, he went into exile. Traveling through Germany, Switzerland, and Italy, he arrived in France where it's said that he performed his "Kantari euskalduna" ("The Basque Singer"), also known as "Gitarra zahartxo bat" ("An Old Guitar"), for Caroline Duprez, the greatest operatic soprano of the day. With that song the two fell passionately in love.

After six years of war, he'd have six years of peace, and—one can hope—love. With Caroline, maybe with others, and certainly with the guitar, with music and poetry. He learned Italian; he learned French. Though he made his living mostly as an itinerant musician, singing in cafés and night clubs, in salons and at private parties, he was also under the financial and political protection of a powerful liberal nobleman.

When the 1848 French Revolution came, he was among those who manned the Paris barricades. From atop the mounds of rubble, he led the singing of the "Marseillaise" to mobilize the people. But as the struggle for Carlos had failed, so too did the revolution. With the coming to power of the new emperor Napoleon III, Joxe Mari found himself on the run again. Caught in Toulouse and arrested there, he was labeled a "subversive element" and thrown out of the country. He fled yet again, this time to England. In London, he visited the Universal Exposition of 1851. He learned English. At one of his performances, the Spanish general José Mazarredo was in the audience. Something of a fan, the general arranged a pardon that would allow the troublesome bard to go home.

Now things get a little murky. Some believe that Joxe Mari returned to Spain in 1851 and went from place to place singing, playing, and reciting poems and songs until 1853 when at the Café de San Luis in Madrid, he performed his "Gernikako arbola" ("The Tree of Gernika") for the first time. He was accompanied on piano by the café's regular musician who wrote the song down. Some even say it was this piano player who composed the melody and that only the words were Iparragirre's. The two men sat side by side at the keyboard. Then it was a couple of years performing in Spain and the Basque Country before Iparragirre was again arrested, this time back home in Gipuzkoa, in Tolosa where, as we learn in "If My Mother Knew," the authorities assured us things would be settled.

In another version of history, Joxe Mari left England and spent two or three years in Central Europe performing with a traveling theater group. Either way, he still ends up at the Café de San Luis in 1853 and still performs "Gernikako arbola" there for the first time.

The two stories converge with Joxe Mari traveling throughout the peninsula performing "Gernikako arbola" which is quickly taken up as a symbol of both the Basque people's bitterness and their hope—anger over the destruction of the foruak and consequent loss of autonomy leavened by dreams of future freedom. Here General Mazarredo reenters the story. It's 1852 and the Tree song is getting worrisomely popular. Mazarredo orders Iparragirre out of the Basque Country. Two years later, during a brief hiccup of progressive politics, Joxe Mari is able to return once again to what in his poems and songs he reminds us is his "beloved Euskal Herria."

But maybe Mazarredo doesn't order the arrest in Tolosa until 1854. It's still about the Tree song and this time when the authorities release Joxe Mari, it's with the understanding that he'll get out of town for good. He hightails it to Santander then travels throughout Spain, playing as he goes. As if unable to read signs of danger, he returns to the Basque Country in the summer of 1855. But he senses something has changed—a certain indifference shown to him by his compatriots, a feeling that he's being watched.

A Spanish senator sent a report to the Madrid government following one of Joxe Mari's concerts, a *plein-air* party somewhere in the rolling folds of the Basque mountains. The Senator wrote: "They announced that Iparragirre would sing 'The Tree of Gernika,' the song that has become the symbol of the Basque Statutes of Autonomy—the foruak. People had gathered from the neighboring farms, villages, and towns—six thousand people. When Iparragirre sang about bowing down to honor the tree, all those six thousand people fell to their knees, leaned forward, and touched their faces to the earth. It was as if the entire crowd had been moved by the force of a spring or the pull of magnetism, a once mindless mass had found a leader and a purpose. When they heard the last verse of the hymn, those men who'd worn the beret for the Pretender Carlos during six years of war, those men of brave heart, well, it sparked a flame in them. They raised their arms in a gesture of pride and swore they would die for Basque freedom."

The Senator finished by noting that despite the fact that Iparragirre's poetry and music arose from generous and noble feelings, and despite the poet's sincere Christian belief, his ardent worship of our Lord, the government acted properly in deporting him. "He has caused such a response among the people that were he allowed to continue it would have been necessary to call in troops to preserve public order and maintain domestic tranquility."

It's exile again, may as well get used to it. Joxe Mari went to America, first to Argentina then to Uruguay. Before leaving Europe, he married a fellow Gipuzkoan—Alegiko Maria Angela Kerexeta. Joxe Mari was 36; Angela 17. Some sources say the marriage took place in February of 1859 which would make Joxe Mari 38. Others say the couple had already embarked before marrying so the wedding must have taken place in Buenos Aires not Gipuzkoa. And the spelling of the bride's name varies from one source to another—María Ángela de Querejeta Aizpurua in one Spanish text. A lovely name. The couple had eight children—six girls and two boys.

Not long after arriving in Buenos Aires, Joxe Mari gave a private concert that was received with great enthusiasm. But when he then gave a large public concert, the enthusiasm was not so great. He and Angela left for Uruguay where he's said to have worked for nearly nineteen years as a sheepherder. Doesn't every Basque in America work as a sheepherder? Some sources make no mention of Iparragirre ever working with sheep.

As the years passed, the author of "Gernikako arbola" was not so much forgotten in the Basque Country as wondered about. Is he dead? That's what most people thought until Ricardo Becerro de Bengoa reported in the September 16, 1876 edition of the newspaper *La Paz* that the bard lived on. A concert was arranged, and a subscription set up to pay for passage across the

Atlantic from Rio de la Plata to Baiona. In 1877, at age 57, but already an old man, Joxe Mari got on the boat, leaving his wife and children behind. Although he landed broke and in bad health, it's never too late for hope and from a hilltop in France looking south, he wrote:

I'm in Hendaia—ecstatic,

eyes wide open, Spain

in sight—no better place

in all of Europe.

But another round of Carlist wars had only recently come to their end, leaving the Basque Country wracked and defeated, the foruak little more than ghosts of memory. Notwithstanding the dizzy happiness Joxe Mari felt coming home, he was demoralized. Let's be honest, he was heartbroken. From that moment on, he would take part only in what he saw as purely cultural events, or efforts to preserve the foruak. He became ever more passionate about Euskara—the Basque language—urging us to speak it everywhere, in town meetings, on the farms, all the time, in shops, on the street, to everyone, in bars and churches.

Given a cash payment by the government of Nafarroa and granted a pension by the governments of Bizkaia, Gipuzkoa, and Araba, Joxe Mari lived as a boarder at a farm in Gabiria, his wife and children still in South America. One day he walked to a roadside inn whose owners were friends. They had dinner. They talked. They recited a few poems, sang a few songs.

It was already dark when Joxe Mari got up to leave. It was raining. Isn't it always raining in Gipuzkoa? There was a bridge, just a little wooden bridge over a narrow stream but the rain was heavy and a channel in a gorge above was overflowing and spilling into the stream making the water rise so it was impossible to cross the low bridge now slippery with water running over it. Joxe Mari tried to ford the stream several times. Unable to cross, he decided to return to his friends' inn. But hours had gone by and when he got there, the windows were shuttered and dark. Everyone was asleep. He took refuge in the pig sty next to the house. Huddled to himself in his soaking clothes, he shivered through the cold night.

The next morning, a servant found Joxe Mari, eyes glazed, teeth chattering, so weak he was unable to get up on his own. They took him into the house, called a doctor who diagnosed pneumonia. For three days Iparragirre got weaker and weaker. He received the Last Rites. He dictated a will, leaving everything to his wife and children. I guess everything would be his guitar. He died on April 6, 1881.

When I began translating Joxe Mari Iparragirre's poems and songs, I knew only "The Tree of Gernika." None of the rest. I worked away, struggling not only to bring nineteenth century Basque into twenty-first century American English, but also to bring Iparragirre's Basque into the contemporary unified Basque—Batua— that is taught in schools and used in the media and the public sphere. Spellings were different, vocabulary was different, verb structure was different. And there was so much Spanish tangled up with the Basque that it would be impossible to translate the work without knowledge of both languages. Iparragirre was very nearly a speaker of what I'd call Euskañol—the mixed Basque Spanish that's akin to Spanglish in the US.

When I think of Iparragirre's place in Basque cultural and political history, I see him as part Walt Whitman, part Woody Guthrie, and part Rumi. He's Whitman, father of modern American poetry, with his embrace of experience and love for everyone when he writes:

> So long, friends,
>
> until that someday
>
> when we meet again.
>
> I'll be the one walking
>
> toward you…

And Whitman is there also in his love of homeland. Walt, from onboard a Yankee clipper, tells us, "My eyes settle the land…I bend at her prow or shout joyously from the deck" while Joxe Mari stands in Hendaia, looking out ecstatically.

He's Woody Guthrie—the voice of working people with a sticker on his guitar reading, "This machine kills fascists," when he sings:

> …let us live
>
> without war
>
> for we've had
>
> all we can take.

In "Back to the Land I Love," he's the Woody of "This Land is Your Land" and "Roll On Columbia, Roll On:"

Over there the beloved mountains,

the rolling fields

and sparkling white farmhouses,

the streams and springs.

Last, he's Jelaluddin Rumi, thirteenth century Sufi mystic, born in Balkh in present day Afghanistan or maybe it was Wakhsh in what's now Tajikistan. Rumi too was a wayfarer, traveling and living in Iran, Iraq, Syria, and Turkey. In Farsi, Arabic, Turkish, and Greek, Rumi spoke above all of union with the beloved. Centuries later, his fellow wayfarer Iparragirre, in Basque, Spanish, French, Italian, and English, also sought to approach the beloved. Lifting his hands over his head Joxe Mari closes his eyes and says,

...I didn't

plan it—this heart's tug.

I wander around hoping

to see you. What a job—

being in love! Driven

crazy thinking of you.

And Rumi with a nod responds,

I didn't come here of my own accord, and I can't leave that way.

Whoever brought me here will have to take me home.

I hope that these translations will help to bring Joxe Mari Iparragirre home to us all, Basque and non-Basque alike.

–David Romtvedt

Buffalo, Wyoming, April, 2020

Joxe Mari Iparragirre
Poems · Bertsoak

Gernikako arbola

Gernikako arbola
Da bedeinkatuba,
Euskaldunen artean
Guztiz maitatuba.
Eman da zabaltzazu
Munduban frutuba;
Adoratzen zaitugu
Arbola santuba.

Mila urte inguru da
Esaten dutela,
Jainkoak jarrizubela
Gernikako arbola.
Zaude bada, zutikan
Orain da denbora,
Eroritzen bazera
Arras galdu gera.

Etzera eroriko,
Arbola maitea,
Baldin portatzen bada
Bizkaiko Juntia.
Laurok artuko degu
Zurekin partia,
Pakian bizi dediñ
Euskaldun jentia.

The Tree of Gernika

Blessed tree
of Gernika,
beloved
by Basques,
fruit given
to the world;
we adore you,
holy tree.

A thousand years
ago, they say, God
planted the tree
of Gernika. If it's
so, now's the time
to stand tall.
Fall and we
lose everything.

But you won't
fall, beloved tree,
as long as Bizkaia
is true.
We four[1] provinces
will be with you,
and the Basques
will live in peace.

Betiko bizi dediñ
Jaunari eskatzeko
Jarri gaitezen danok
Laister belauniko.
Eta biotzetikan
Ezkatu ezkero,
Arbola biziko da
Oraiñ eta gero.

Arbola botatzia
Dutela pentzatu
Euskal-erri guziyan
Denak badakigu.
Ea bada jendia,
Denbora orain degu
Erori gabetanik
Iruki biagu.

Betiko egongo zera
Uda berrikoa
Lore aintziñetako
Mantza gabekua.
Errukizaitez bada
Biotz gurekua,
Denbora galdu gabe
Emanik frutuba.

Arbolak erantzun du
Kontuz bizitzeko
Eta biotzetikan
Jaunari eskatzeko;
Gerrarik nai ez degu
Pakea betiko
Gure lege zuzenak
Emen maitatzeko.

On our knees
let's ask God
to give our tree
eternal life,
and if we ask
sincerely, it
will be so, now
and forever.

Listen, we know
some in Spain
would cut the tree
down. People,
we know this.
There's not much
time to keep it
standing.

Summer's eternal
gift, unblemished
timeless flower.
If you pity us,
pity our hearts,
do not delay
in giving us
your fruit.

The tree says
if you want
peace, not war,
wake up!
Ask God
from your heart,
love the true
old laws.

Erregutu diogun
Jaungoiko Jaunari
Pakea emateko
Oraiñ eta beti.
Bai eta indarrare
Zedorren lurrari,
Eta bendiziyoa
Euskal-erriari.

Orain kanta ditzagun
Lau bat bertso berri
Gure probintziaren
Alabantza garri.
Arabak esaten du
Su garrez beterik
Nere biotzekua
Eutsiko diat nik.

Gipuzkoa urrena
Arraz zentiturik
Asi da deadarrez
Ama Gernikari.
Erori etzaitezen
Arrimatu neri
Zure zendogarriya
Emen naukazu ni.

Ostoa berdia ta
Zañak ere fresko
Nere seme maiteak
Ez naiz eroriko.
Beartzen banaiz ere
Egon beti pronto
Nigandikan etsayak
Itsulitzareko.

Let us pray
to God above
for peace, now
and always,
that our land
be strong, and
that the Basque
Country be blessed.

And let us sing
four new songs
to praise our four
provinces. Araba,
on fire, promises,
"I will be true
to what I carry
in my heart."

Then Gipuzkoa,
all feeling, calling,
"Mother Gernika,
come close to me
so you don't fall.
I am your trunk,
here to hold
you up."

"My dear children,
I will not fall—my
leaves are green,
my roots new.
But if I call, be
ready to drive
our enemies
from me."

Guztiz maitagarria
Eta oestargiña
Begiratu gaitzazu
Zeruko erregiña.
Gerrarik gabetanik
Bizi albagiña
Oraiñdaño izan degu
Guretzako diña.

Queen of the sky,
most worthy
of love and honor,
watch over us,
let us live
without war
for we've had
all we can take.

Nere amak baleki

Zibilak esan naute
Biziro egoki
Tolosan biar dala
Gauza erabaki.
Giltzapian sartu naute
Poliki poliki
Negar egingo luke
Nere amak baleki.

Jesus tribunalian
Sutenian sartu
Etziyon Pilatosek
Kulparik bilatu.
Neri ere arkitu
Ez dirate barkatu
Zergatik ez dituzte
Eskubak garbitu?

Kartzelatik aterata
Fiskalaren etxera
Abisatu ziraten
Juateko beriala.
Ez etortzeko geyago
Probintzi onetara
Orduan artu nuan
Santander-aldera.

If My Mother Knew

The authorities[2] tell me,
as only they can,
to be ready, tomorrow
in Tolosa things
will be settled.
They locked me up.[3]
If my mother knew,
she'd cry.

When Jesus
was brought
to trial, Pilate
found him innocent.
I, too, am innocent
yet unpardoned.
Why haven't they
washed their hands?

Released from jail,
they urged me
to report to the
prosecutor's office
and get out
of Gipuzkoa forever.
With that in mind
I took off for Santander.

Kantari euskalduna

Gitarra zartxo bat da
Neretzat laguna;
Onela ibiltzen da
Artista euskalduna:
Egun batean pobre,
Beste batez jauna,
Kantari pasatzen det
Nik beti eguna.

Naiz dala Italia,
Oro bat Francia
Bietan bilatu det
Anitz malizia.
Ikusten badet ere
Nik mundu guzia
Beti maitatuko det
Euskalerria.

Jaunak ematen badit
Neri osasuna,
Izango det oraindik
Andregai bat ona.
Emen badet frantzesa
Interesa duna,
Baña nik naiago det
Utzik euskalduna.

The Basque Singer

An old guitar
my only friend.
Here's how it goes
for the Basque musician:
broke one minute,
a gentleman the next.
Either way, I spend
the day singing.

I might be in Italy
but it's the same
in France—malice
and deceit.
Let's say I see
the whole world—
it'll always be
Euskal Herria[4] I love.

If the Lord grants
me good health,
a good woman
will still have me.
Like this French one—
rich. But honestly,
I'd prefer a Basque
girl—scruffy, broke.

Agur Euskal-Erria
Baña ez betiko
Bost edo sei urtetan
Ez det ikusiko.
Jaunari eskatzen diot
Grazia emateko
Nere lur maite ontan
Ezurrak uzteko.

Farewell, Euskal Herria.
I won't see you
for five maybe six years.
Well, it's not forever.
Here's my last request—
Lord take pity on me,
let my bones rest
in my beloved homeland.

Nere maitearentzat

Ume eder bat ikusi nuen
Donostiako kalean,
Itz erditxo bat ari esan gabe
Nola pasatu parean?
Gorputza zuan liraina eta
Oinak zebiltzen aidean,
Politagorik ez det ikusi
Nere begien aurrean.

Aingeru zuri, pare gabea,
Euskalerriko alaba,
Usterik gabe zugana beti
Nere biotzak narama.
Ikusi naian beti or nabil,
Nere maitea, au lana!
Zoraturikan emen naukazu
Beti pentsatzen zugana.

Galai gazteak galdetzen dute,
Aingeru on nun ago?
Nere maitea nola deitzen dan
Ez du inortxok jakingo;
Ez berak ere ez luke naiko,
Konfiantza orretan nago.
Amoriodun biotz oberik
Euskalerrian ez dago.

For My Beloved

I saw a beauty
on a Donostia street.
How could I pass
and not speak?
She was slender,
and her walk—
I'd never seen
lovelier steps.

Bright angel beyond
compare, daughter
of Euskadi. I didn't
plan it—this heart's tug.
I wander around hoping
to see you. What a job—
being in love! Driven
crazy thinking of you!

The don Juans ask,
"Where's the angel?"
Not one of us knows
even her name and
I'm sure that's how
she wants it. No
more loving heart,
not around here.

Nere ongille maiteei

Ez dakit nola eskerrak eman
Ah! nere ongille maiteak
Nere lurrera bear nau eraman
Gaur zuen borondateak;
Egin dezute zer obra ona
Aberatz eta pobreak
Orra kunplitu agintzen duana
Jesukristoren legeak.

Biotz oneko jaunak badira,
Lista dutenak edertzen
Zori oneko nere zartzera
Ah! nola duten onratzen;
Munduan bada zorionikan,
Andre onak du egiten,
Gizonak izar oyetan
Zerua degu ikusten.

O! zu Romero Jimenez jauna,
Nere adiskide maitea,
Zure biotz onak kontsolatu du
Nere anima tristea;
Egiak dira nere ametsak:
Mendietara joatea;
Agur, Romero, au da neretzat
Gozamentu eta pakea.

To Those Who've Helped Me

How can I thank
those who've helped me,
whose kindness must
carry me home.
Good work done
by rich and poor,
what a fine thing—
to follow Christ's way.

Honored to be on
the list with men
of great heart, I admit
it's luck. If there's
happiness on earth,
it's made by a woman,
the star through which
a man sees the sky.

You, Mr. Romero Jiménez,[5]
dear friend, good heart,
who consoles my worn soul.
My dreams come true—
to return to the mountains.
This goodbye, Romero,
brings me sweet
pleasure and peace.

Agur, zuri, Olaso jauna,
Bizkaitar prestu noblea;
Beti betiko zure izena
Biotzean det gordea.
Gaztetanik zait gusta biziki
Mendietako aizea;
Agur, banoa, nai det ikusi
Euskal-erri maitea.

And goodbye to you,
Mr. Olaso, of Bizkaia—
upright, noble, your name
engraved on my heart.
From my first days this
mad love of the mountain wind.
Goodbye, I'm going, longing
to see my beloved Euskal Herria.

Agur Euskalerriari

Gazte gaztetatikan
Erritik kanpora
Estranjeri aldean
Pasa det denpora;
Egiya alde guzietan
Toki onak badira
Baña biotzak dio
Zuaz euskalerrira.

Lur maitea emen ustea
Da negargarria
Emen gelditzen dira
Ama eta erria;
Urez noa ikustera
Bai, mundu berria
Oraintxen bai naizela
Errukigarria.

Agur nere biotzeko
Amatxo maitea
Laister etorriko naiz
Konsola zaitean;
Jaungoikoak nahi badu
Ni urez joatea
Ama zertarako da
Negar egitea?

Greetings, Euskal Herria

Just a kid, I took off
for foreign lands.
I've spent my time
here and there,
and while it's true
there's good everywhere,
my heart tells me
to go home.

The land I love,
it's right here—
my mother, my
friends—I could cry.
I cross the ocean
to see the New World.
Now look at me—
it's pathetic.

So long, beloved
mother of my heart.
I keep in mind
that, God willing,
I'll soon cross
the ocean again.
So why cry, mother,
what for?

Gora euskera

Espaiñian da gizon bat
Bear deguna maita
Franzisko Aizkibel jauna
Euskaldunen aita:
Txit da gizon prestua
Eta jakintzua
Errespeta desagun
Guk gure maitasua.

Ogeita geyo urtian
Bizi da Toledo'n
Izarraizko semia
Ez da beti lo egon;
Liburuen gañian
Beti gau eta egun,
Gure euskera maitia
Galdu ez desagun.

Arabe eta hebreo
Denak denak bera,
Nere adiskideak:
Gora, gora euskera!
Biotzean gurutza,
Eskuan bandera,
Esan lotsarik gabe
Euskaldunak gera!

Wagging the Basque Tongue

There's a man in Spain
we should love—
the Honorable Mister
Franzisko Aizkibel,[6]
father of the Basques,
most worthy and wise.
Let's respect
our teacher.

Child of Izarraitz,
he's lived in Toledo
more than twenty years.
Never sleeps.
Night and day,
bent over his books
so we won't lose
our beloved tongue.

Arabic and Hebrew—
all languages, friends,
worthy. Euskara, too,
may it live on—
cross in our hearts,
flag in our hands.
So go ahead, say it—
euskaldunak gara.[7]

Pakean bizitzeko
Gure mendietan
Euskera itz egin bear da
Batzarre denetan;
Ta euskaldunen izena
Geroko eunkietan
Famatua izango da
Alde guzietan.

To live at peace
in our mountains,
we've got to speak
Basque wherever
we meet. Centuries
will pass and still,
all the earth will
know our name.

Nere etorrera lur maitera

I

Ara nun diran mendi maiteak
Ara nun diran zelayak
Baserri eder zuri zuriak
Iturri eta ibayak.

Endaian nago zoraturikan
Zabal zabalik begiak
Ara España... lur oberikan
Ez du Europa guziak.

II

Gero pozik bai Donostira
Okendo-ren aurrera
Zeru polit au utzi bearra
Nere anayak, au pena!

Iru txulueta maitagarria
Lore tokiya zu zera
Beneziaren grazi guztiak
Gaur Donostian dira.

Back to the Land I Love

I

Over there the beloved mountains,
the rolling fields
and sparkling white farmhouses,
the streams and springs.

I'm in Hendaia—ecstatic,
eyes wide open, Spain
in sight—no better place
in all of Europe.

II

Then to Donostia, happy
before Okendo's[8] image.
It hurts, brothers, to be
driven from Paradise.

Irutxulu, a garden
casting your spell—
the grace of Venice
here in Donostia.

III

Oh, Euskalerri eder maitea
Ara emen zure semea
Bere lurrari muñ egitera
Beste gabe etorria.

Zuregatikan emango nike
Pozik, bai biziya
Beti zuretzat il arteraño
Gorputz eta anima guzia.

IV

Agur bai Donostiako
Nere anai maiteak
Bilbao-tikan izango dira
Aita zarraren berriak.

Eta gañera itz neurtuetan
Garbi esanez eginak
Sud-Amerikan zer pasatzen dan
Jakiñ dezaten erriak.

III

Oh, lovely beloved
Euskal Herria, here's
your son, home to bow
and kiss your face.

For you, I would give
my life, yes, gladly
for you, unto death,
body and soul.

IV

But goodbye for now,
beloved brothers of Donostia
From Bilbao you'll get news
of the old father.

I'll send word—in poetry!—
images so clear that even
over there you'll see what's
going on in South America.

Glu, glu, glu…

Biba Rioja, Biba Naparra
Arkume onaren iztarra
Emen guztiok anaiak gera
Ustu dezagun pitzarra.

Glu, glu, glu…

Ardo fiña ta jateko ona
Jartzen badute gaur ugari,
Gure barrenak berdindurikan
Jarriko dira guri, guri.

Glu, glu, glu…

Gure zabela bete bear da
Albada gauza onarekiñ,
Dagon lekutik, eragiñ bapo!
Aupa mutilak! gogoz ekiñ.

Glu, glu, glu…

Ez ikaratu dagon artean
Jan eta edan gaur gogotik,
Ustutzen bada ekarko degu
Berriro lengoko tokitik

Glu, glu, glu…

Umoria da gauzik onena
Nai gabeak ditu astutzen,
Uju ta aja asi gaitean
Euskal doñuak kantatutzen.

Glu, glu, glu…

Glub, Glub, Glub...

Viva Rioja! Viva Nafarroa!
A good leg of lamb.
One big happy family.
Drink up, brothers!

Glub, glub, glub...

Good food, fine wine—
if they fill the table,
we'll fill our guts,
get roaring drunk.

Glub, glub, glub...

We'll eat till we burst,
the best we can get,
wherever it's from.
Come on, boys, dig in!

Glub, glub, glub...

Don't fear tomorrow.
Eat, drink, and be merry!
All gone? There's more
where that came from.

Glub, glub, glub...

Good cheer—that's the ticket.
It strips away the pain
so let's belt out the old
Basque songs, starting now.

Glub, glub, glub...

Nere izarra

Zu zera nere izarra
Zu nere eguzkia
Aingeruen artetik
Zerutik jatxia.

Barren kalera nua
Bertan nai det bizi,
Antxen ikusiko det
Sarritan Maiñazi.

Nere biotza dago
Oso penaturik,
Joan bear detalako
Laister zure ondotik.

Zure ondoren nabil
Erdi txoraturik
Nere biotz gaisoa
Ezin sendaturik.

Zure amorio gabe,
Ai! nere Maiñazi!
Ez det mundu onetan
Geiago nai bizi.

Goizetikan gabera
Emen nago itxoten
Nere izar txuria ez
Da oraindik agertzen.

Alfer alferrik dabiltz
Zozuak kantari,
Ai! nere Maiñazitxok
Ez du nai etorri.

My star

You are my star,
my sun, the one
angel come down
from Heaven.

I'm moving to High
Street. That's where
I'll live, where I'm
sure to see Maiñazi.[9]

The painful crack
in my heart will
only get wider—
having to leave you.

Walking beside you,
half mad with love.
Can't repair
a broken heart.

Oh, hell, Maiñazi,
without you,
why go on living
in this world?

I spend the night
waiting but my
shining star
doesn't appear.

This insane crow
goes on singing.
Not that Maiñazi
will ever come.

Zugana Manuela

Zugana, Manuela
Nuanian pensatu
Uste det ninduala
Deabruak tentatu,
Ikusi beziñ ekiñ
Naiz enamoratu
Ojala ez baziñan
Sekulan agertu.

Amorioz beterik
Esperantza gabe,
Zergatik egin ziñan
Biotz onen jabe,
Zuk esan bihar zenduben
Emendikan alde
Egiyaz ez naiz ni
Bizar dunen zale.

Aztu nai zaitut baña
Eziñ, eziñ aztu,
Zure amoriyuak
Buruba dit galdu;
Oraiñ bigundu zenduke
Eta maitagarri orrek
Biotz on bihundu
Piska bat lagundu.

About You, Manuela

When I think
about you, Manuela,
I'm pretty sure
it was the devil
tempting me.
Love at first sight,
they say. If only
I hadn't seen you.

It's hopeless, this
love. Why'd you
pick my heart
to rule? Better
to have said,
"Buzz off, truth
is I never liked
men with beards."

I want to forget
you but can't.
I've gone soft
in the head.
How about you
soften your heart
a little, help
love along?

Barkatu bear dituzu
Nere erkeriak
Sure begira daude
Nere bi begiyak;
Garbi, garbi esan ditut
Nere ustes egiak
Soraturikan nauka
Sure arpegiak.

Gabian ibilli naiz
Guzizko ametsetan
Donostian nengoela
Andre marietan;
Eta ikusi nubela
Erri artako plazan
Erdiyan zebillela
Manuelatxo dantzan.

Forgive my
blurting this out,
my eyes drawn
to yours. Look,
to speak plainly,
it's like this—
I see your face
and go crazy.

Every night
the same dream—
Donostia,
the celebration
of the Virgin Mary,
and in the square,
Manuela,
dancing.

Errukaria

Aspaldien ezta gure etxean
Ogirik ikusi,
Bañan gaur txitxi ta parra
Izango da noski.

> Gaur bai jana ta edana
> Labiru lena
> Jango ote degu dana
> Labiru la. Ju!

Oso arlote bizi gera,
Ezin osaturik;
Zenbat aldiz eguerdian
Oraindik baraurik.

> Gaur bai jana ta edana...

Marto opillak egiteko,
Arto egiteko,
Aitak atzo saldu zuen
Anega bat arto.

> Gaur bai jana ta edana...

Talo esnea jateko gu
Gaude zaleturik;
Sei talo jango nituzke
Neronek bakarrik.

> Gaur bai jana ta edana...

Needy

It's a long time without
a scrap of bread in the house.
But today—all we can eat.
And laughter.

        Yes, food and drink today.
        La bi ru la lay.
        We'll eat it all, I say.
        La bi ru la, hey!

It's a raggedy-ass life.
Nothing to be done. Noon
and I haven't had a bite.
Let's just say I'm fasting.

        Yes, food and drink today...

Yesterday for the baby's
christening father sold
a bushel and a half of corn
to grind some flour.

        Yes, food and drink today...

We love corn tortillas
with cream of anything soup.
Corn tortillas! I could
eat six myself.

        Yes, food and drink today...

Gure sabelak eske daude
Au da miseria
Erdi gosiak dagona
Da errukarria.

      Gaur bai jana ta edana...

Pitxarra ere guretzako
Izango da noski,
Gure barrena alai
Jarriko da aurki.

      Gaur bai jana ta edana...

Reduced to begging,
stomachs growling,
miserable, half starved.
It's pathetic.

    Yes, food and drink today…

That jug on the table—
of course, it's for us!
We're feeling good,
sucking it down.

    Yes, food and drink today…

Amerikatik,

Urretxuako semiei

Billarreal de Urretxu
Nere erri maitea
Seme bat emen dezu
Amorioz betea.
Nai, baña nola ikusi
Au da lan tristea
Zuretzat nai det bizi
Urretxu nerea.

Bi milla eta seiregun
Legua badira,
Montebideotikan
Euskal errira
Naiz esperantzetan
Etorri bagera
Aurreratasun gabe
Urtiak juan dira.

Bai, nere adiskideak
Bear da pensatu
Zuretzat Amerikak
Nola dan mudatu
Iñork emen eziñ du
Lanikan billatu
Oraiñ datorrenari
Bear zaio damutu.

From America,
to the People of Urretxu

Billareal de Urretxu— [10]
home sweet home—
here's your native son
full of love, longing
to see you. But how?
It's grim work, my
Urretxu, wanting
to live for you.

Six thousand miles
from Euskal Herria
to Montevideo.
While we came
here full of hope,
the years have
passed and we've
gotten nowhere.

Keep in mind,
friends, how
much America
has changed.
No one can find
work. Show up
now and you're
bound to regret it.

Gañera izan degu
Emen ere gerra
Gure zori onean
Pakea egiñ da;
Bañan gerra ondoren
Dakar diktadura
On Lorenzo Latorre
Nagusi degula.

Ez, bada, ez etorri
Gaur lur onetara
Il edo bizi obe da
Juatea Habanara;
Au da gure bandera
Españaren onra
Txurrukaren semeak
Ara juango gera.

Agur adiskideak
Ikusi artean
Zuenganatuko naiz
Egunen batean.
Esperantzakin bizi
Nai det bitartean
Gero ezurrak utzi
Nere lur maitean.

On top of which
there's war here, too,
although—lucky us!—
they've declared
peace under
a dictatorship
run by
don Lorenzo Latorre.[11]

So, look, don't
come to this country.
Living or dead, better
to head for Havana
with Txurruka's children,[12]
Spain's honor, the flag
nailed to the mast.
Yes, let's go there.

So long, friends,
until that someday
when we meet again.
I'll be the one walking
toward you. Meanwhile,
I live hoping that
in the end my bones
will rest at home.

Mairuen bandera

Nafarrak On Garcia
Errege zutela
Odolez estali zan
Bai Balde-Junkera.
Afrikanoak orruz...
Legoiak bezela
Zioten kristau bizirik
Utzi bear ez zala.

Baña Euskaldunak
Laurak-Bat aurrera!
Zioten: Fedeagatik
Danok ilko gera;
Jo!... jo eta ez eman
Pauso bat atzera...
Gurea izan arte
Mairuen bandera.

Mutillak... ara non dan
Illargi erdia,
Arrapatu dezagun
Naiz galdu bizia:
Emen degu bandera
Upa Euskal-erria!
Eta Anzuolarentzat
Onra ta gloria.

The Muslim Flag

When the Navarrese
had don Garcia[13] as king,
Balde-Junkera
was covered in blood.
The Africans roared
like lions, no
Christian to be
left alive.

But the Basques—
forward the four[14]
saying, "For the faith
we'll die, blow
upon blow, never
a step back until
the Muslim flag
is ours."

There, boys,
the crescent moon.
Let's grab it though
we lose our lives.
We have it. Take
heart, Euskal Herria,
honor and glory
for Antzuola.[15]

San Juan Uzarragako
Seme txit argiak
Ziran Balde-Junkeran
Irabaz larriak;
Batzar etxean dauden
Illargi erdiak
Dira Anzuolarentzat
Txit onrragarriak.

Esan adiskideak
Orduan bezela
Nafarrakin gaur ere
Anaiak gerala;
Bat da gure izarra
Bat gure bandera
Esan beti Laurak-Bat
Izan nai degula.

Eskribitze mesede
Egiten banauzu
Gabiriara karta
Bidal bear duzu.
An baserri batean
Beti triste nauzu
Buruan ditudala
Mila pentsamendu.

At Balde-Junkera,
the clear sighted
people of Uzarraga[16]
carried the day,
the crescent moon
now in the town hall
of Antzuola, great
honor to all.

Say, friends,
as of old, we're
one with Navarre,
the four provinces—
one star, one flag.
Say always, four
as one, what
we want to be.

If it occurs to you
to write, send your
letter—that kindness—
to Gabiria.[17] I'll be
staying on a farm
there—sad, I admit—
a thousand thoughts
spinning in my head.

Jaungoikoa eta arbola

Fueristak gera, eta izango,
Mundua mundu dan artean;
Sentimentu au bizirik dago
Betiko Euskalerrian,
Naiz eri izan gure anima,
Gaude soseguz bakean;
Ikusiko da gure arbola
Zutik egunen batean.

Mendietako raza noblea
Gaur buru makur begira:
Beti izan da fueroen legea
Euskaldunen anima.
Argitasunik ez da ageri;
Zerua dago iluna;
Libertadea esan kantari
Il arte maita dugula.

Zoaz, D. Karlos Zazpigarrena,
Urrun bai gure lurretik;
Ez dezu uzi guretzat pena
Eta tristura besterik;
Lutoz negarrez ama gaisoak,
Ay! ezin konsolaturik;
Ez degu nai ez geiago ikusi
Zori gaiztoko gerrarik.

God and the Tree

We're fueristas[18] and,
while the earth turns,
will be. This feeling
is alive in Euskadi.
Though our soul aches,
we're at ease, certain
that one day we'll see
our tree standing tall.

Once noble people
of the mountains, now
ground down. The old
laws are the Basque soul.
There's no light, the sky
dark. You singer, tell
them we love liberty,
will die for liberty.

Away, King Carlos
the Seventh, go.
You leave us nothing
but pain and sorrow,
distraught mothers
weeping for the dead,
inconsolable. Enough
with your rotten wars.

Euskaldun onak bear du eriotza
Bila bere sorlekuan;
Lurra da ama; maitatzen bada,
Sartuko zera zeruan;
Sinistu, maita, izan fedea
Gure liburu santuan,
Eta arbola biba orain eta
Eriotzako orduan.

Amodiozko lege santuakin,
Gorroto gabe biotzean,
Iberiako gure anaiekin
Bizi nai degu bakean.
Gure izatea eta ondasunak
Dira arbola maitean.
Libertadea maita dutenak
Betoz gurekin batera.

Egunen batez agertuko da
Gure goizeko izarra...
Bere odoietan inguru dela
Jaun Zuriaren itzala,
Eta orduan zainetan bada
Ibero zarren odola
Biziak eman esanez biba
Jaungoikoa eta arbola.

Arren! ez bada galdu esperantza
Gerturatzen da eguna
Nazioen liga edo alianza
Da ikusiko duguna.
Orduan gora Kriston legea
Errespetatzen duguna.
Bai, Euskaldunen borondatea
Da errien anaitasuna.

True Basques will die
where they were born.
The earth is our mother.
If we love her, we
enter heaven. Believe,
love, be true to the holy
book, and may our tree
live even unto death.

Under love's sacred
rule, with hearts free
of hate, we would live
in peace with our
fellow Iberians,[19] our
being, our wellbeing,
in the tree. Want to be
free? Come with us.

One day our morning star
will rise, the shadow
of Jaun Zuria[20] among
the clouds. Then, if
the blood of the old
Iberians runs in our veins,
we'll give our lives crying,
"for God and the tree."

I beg you, don't lose hope.
The day
is coming when
we'll see a league
of nations, when
Christ's law will rule.
Yes, Basque grit
is our country's glue.

Nere oldozmena

Betiko nere religioa da
Adoratzea iru gauza,
Jainkoa, lurra ta familia
Da nere urreko ametsa.

Baña, au lana! Lurra naiean
Pil pil da nere biotza
Ezurrak ditut noski lurrean
Laster usteko esperantza.

Thinking About It

Ok, in my religion
we worship three things—
God, mother earth,
and family. That's it.

But what a job! My heart
banging away for home.
That's where my bones
will lie. Anyway, I hope.

Nabarrako Euzko Bazkunari

Zorioneko batzar onetan
Nabarrak gure anaiak,
Bizi dirade lege onean
Gaur guztiz gizon ernayak
Guregatik on esango badu
Etorkizunak kondairak
Laurak bat beti... maite alkartu
Izan euskaldun leyalak.

Alkar gaitezen txiki ta aundi
Aberats eta pobreak
Maita zaiteste, esaten digu
Jaungoikoaren legeak.
Auziak utsi alde batera
Batu euskaldun guziak
Besoak zabal esaten digu
Gaur Iruña erriak.

Erruki zaite, oh, Jaun maitea!
Lagundu Euskalerria
Bada guztiok alkartu gera
Oraiñ beltz eta zuriya
Anai arteko guda beti da
Guztizko negargarriya
Arren anayak errespetatu
Gizon guztien biziya.

To the Basque Association
of Navarre

A great meeting we had
with our compatriots
from Nafarroa![21] They're
sharp, their laws just.
Historians of the future
will say, "Well done—
the four[22] can be one,
honest to God Basques."

Young, old, rich, poor,
let's come together.
Love—it's God's
only law. Today
in Iruña[23] they met us,
arms spread wide,
saying, "Come on,
enough arguing."

Lord, have mercy,
help Euskal Herria
come together—
Black and White—[24]
for in a civil war
we all cry. Sisters,
brothers, please,
respect all lives.

Oroitza

Elizondoko uri
Eder politean
Euskalduna ugari
Bildu da pakian,
Esanez batu gara
Bai zori onean
Gorrotorik gaur ezta
Gure batzarrean.

Nafarren elkargoa
Burutzat degula
Zer zori onekoak
Maitatzen bagera,
Euskaldun on guztiak
Zerura begira
Ezan euskalerria
Salbatu dedilla,

Mundu berrian ere
Gaur euskaldun onak
Nai gabetuak daude
Biotza dutenak
Galtzen gure euskera
Onra eta oiturak
Arren ez galdu doaiak!
Jainkoak emanak.

Remembering

In beautiful Elizondo[25]
the Basque flocks
have gathered,
united in peace,
saying all for one,
no hard feelings.
Yes, no hatred
in today's meeting.[26]

If we love one
another, good
fortune will follow—
Nafarroa's the model.
True Basques look
to the sky that
Euskal Herria
be saved.

In America, too,
sorrow now marks
those who remain
Basque at heart—
language, customs,
name—disappearing.
Please, don't abandon
what God has given.

Nafarren bide onak
Gaur laurak batean
Da artu bear dana
Errien onean,
Euskaldun on guztiak
Betiko pakean
Eztegu nai gudarik
Anayen artean.

Nafarroa's way—
the four as one—
must be our way.
Now! For the good
of the nation, good
of the people. Peace!
No more war, no more
Basque killing Basque.

Galdu genduen gure Moraza

Zan Mateo Benigno
Moraza on jauna
Euskalerri guziak
Maita genduena,
Prestua, jakintsua
A zer biotz ona
Jaungoikoak zerura
Eraman ziguna!

Bitoriako semeak
Ernai ta nobleak
Guztiz maita zituan
Fueroko legeak,
Galdu ziradenean
Zer naigabeak
Bizia galdu arte
Moraza maiteak.

Guk ere bear degu
Morazak bezela
Esan beti ill arte
Fedea degu ta
Gure Jaungoiko onak
Laguntzen digula
Noiz bat... Euskalerria
Salbatuko dala.

Moraza is Dead

Mateo Benigno Moraza[27]
is dead. Loved by all
in Euskal Herria.
A big hearted, wise,
and decent man.
God has taken him
from us, carried him
off to Heaven.

Child of Gasteiz,[28]
noble watchman
who loved the old
laws. And when
they were gone,
it dogged him
to the end of his life.
Our Moraza!

We should be
like him, say again
and again, unto
death, we have faith,
the good Lord will
help us, will save
Euskal Herria.
One day.

Obian

Euskalerria maite zuanaren
Orra nun degun obia
Lur santu on jartzera goazen
Lore koroez betia,
Igo zan zeruetara
Bitoriar prestu noblea
Bere izena gure biotzetan
Izan betiko gordea.

Galdu genduen gure Moraza
Baña bizi da izena
Laurak batentzat zan esperantza
Biotz nobleko gizona,
Gorde dezagun bere oroitza
Euskaldun onak bagera
Lur onegatik gure biotza
Eman Morazak bezela.

Amoriozko txit bide ona
Berak lur oni emana
Da euskaldunak betikoeran
Idurikatu beardana
Egun obe bat ez da urruti
Alkar maitatzen degula
Gure mendietan biziko gera
Anai maitiak bezela.

Graveside

There's the grave
of one who loved
Euskal Herria—sacred
ground. Let's cover it
with flowers, a crown
for the dead, deep soul
of Gasteiz, risen to Heaven,
his name in our hearts.

Moraza is dead
but he lives on.
The great man's hope?
That the four be one.
Let's remember him
and if we're truly Basque,
give our hearts, as he
did, for this land.

Love of place, the road
he showed us, forever
Basque. Better days
aren't so far away.
Love one another
and we'll live on
in our mountains.
One family. Imagine!

Okendori

Zeruetan jarri al banezake
Gaur Okendoren izena
Biotz guztitik jasoko nuke
Alderakedan bezela,
Baña zer lana au neretzako
Ezagueraz naiz laburra
Bear bezala ondo neurtzeko
Bere kondaira ederra.

Ogei ta zazpi urte zituala
Zan Gipuzka-tar azkarra
Etsaiak larri artzen zituana
Eman ezkero aupada
Betiko onra Españarena
Itxasoetan bakarra
Eta munduan bere aomena
Odoiaz goiti dagoena.

Zenbait ibilli eta jazarra
Cadiz-en eta Lisboan!
Errendituak zenbait gudari
Antonio-ren menpean!
Asko alditan Olandesakin
Eta mairuen artean
Bildurra zer zan ez jakin
Okendoren biotzean.

The Thing About Okendo

If I could I would,
with all my heart,
put Okendo's name
in the sky. But
what a job! My
clumsy words!
To tell his grand
story as I should.

He was twenty-seven—
a capable Gipuzkoan
who, when confronted,
drove the enemy down.
Always for Spain's honor,
lord of the seas, and
on earth, a memory
rising with the clouds.

So much action and
turmoil in Cadiz and
in Lisbon. So many
enemy troops taken,
tangling with the Dutch
and the North Africans.
He didn't know
the word fear.

Kantauriako ontzi guztien
Agintari zan Okendo
Ibiltzen zana itxasoetan
Aizea bezin agudo
Ala jantzan Brasil aldera
Donarioz eta garboso
Esanez «goazen etsaien billa
Diran lekuan eraso».

Ara nun dauden esaten zuan
Eman deiogun arpegi
Gogor... bakoitza bere lekuan
Su... su ill arte ez utzi
Ez oraindikan ez du etsaiak
Nere bizkarrik ikusi
Agertuko da jazar ondoren
Emen zeiñ geran nagusi.

Asi ziraden sutan bertatik
Eta Auspaster aundiak
Eraso zion gogor albotik
Orduan ziran larriak
Baña Okendo beti azkarrak
Oso suturik begiak
An ekiñ zion su eta garra
Zati eginez ontziak.

Olandesak an eztu artuak
Larritazunak an ziran
Geienak seatu
Itxasoren erdian
Ontziak ere su artu zuten
Ondatutzeko zorian
Okendo bera zan errukitzen
Nai gabetasun aundian.

Commander of the
Cantabrian ships,
he skimmed the seas
quick as the wind,
to Brazil, a storm,
saying, "We'll track
the enemy, attack
wherever they are."

"Wherever they are,"
he said, "show them
our faces. To your
places! Fire! Till all
are dead. No enemy
has seen my back.
Battle done, we'll be
here—victorious."

Then, the real battle,
the fires, the great
Hauspaster[29] driving hard
from the side, a dark
moment, but Okendo,
quick, eyes blazing,
fighting tooth and nail,
splintered the enemy ships.

And the Dutch,
trapped, were beaten.
The men, most of them,
lost at sea, ships, too,
burning, going down.
Seeing such loss,
even Okendo knew
pity and regret.

Ala dakite gizon biotz dunak
Errendituari barkatzen
Egi au bera bai euskaldunak
Gudari bada izaten
Izan gaitezen danok anaiak
Eta alkartu gaitezen.
O! ez ibilli euskal leialak
Lurrak odolez eztaltzen.

Izanik garailaria
Arrotasunik ez zuan
Ala zan gure gizon aundia
Jazar lekuan berean
Burua zutik, begiak argi
Eta ezpatia eskuan,
Ematen zuan beti arpegi
Argidotarren moduan.

Fededun ona beti izana
Eta gudari aundia beregana
Jaungoikoak deitu zuan
Gizon illezkor argia
Alabatua bere izena
Gaur zeruetan jarria
Bere gloriaz bete zuana
Betiko Euskalerria.

Those of good heart
pardon the defeated.
Basque warriors know
this truth. Let's admit
we are brothers, be as one.
Oh, you faithful Basques,
stop! Stop covering
the earth in blood.

He took no pride
in victory, this
good man. Even
in the heat of battle—
head high, clear eyed,
sword in hand,
facing the world
like the heroes of old.

Ever faithful, great
warrior called to God.
Bright immortal,
praise his name,
his boundless light
shining in the Heavens,
reflecting glory
on Euskal Herria.

Bezerro Bengoa, Arrese, Erran eta Manteleri

Erran, Manteli, Arrese jauna
Eta Bezerro Bengoa
Badet aspaldi biotz guztitik
Ezagutzeko gogua.

Zuek bezela ditut maitatzen
Jaungoikoa eta Fueroak
Ay! baña ez nau pakean usten
Lurraren amorioak.

Itxaso aldera beti begira
Zabal zabalik begiak
Oh, Jaun maitea, zer urriñ diran
Euskal erriko mendiak.

Ara ontzi bat, goazen atozte.
Nere aur polit gaisoak
Bildurrik gabe juan zaiteste
Txit maite gaitu Jainkoak.

Mundu zarrean nola berrian
Izan gaitezen prestuak
Gizonarentzat agiñ zituan
Ur eta lurrak Jainkoak

Zabaldu beti anaitasuna
Amoriozko kantuak
Guzientzat du itzal ederra
Gure arbola santuak.

Note to Bezerro Bengoa, Arrese, Herran, and Manteli

To Misters Herran, Manteli,
Arrese, and Bezerro Bengoa.[30]
For so long and with all my heart
I've wanted to meet you.

Like you I love God
and the foruak,[31] but
oh, my love of place
gives me no ease.

Eyes peeled, ceaselessly
staring across the sea.
Dear God, the Basque
mountains so far away.

A boat home—get on board,
my beautiful unfortunate
children. Have no fear.
God holds us dear.

She made the earth
and the sea—for us.
Old World and New—
let's do what's right.

Sow eternal good will,
love's song. Room
for all in the boundless
shade of our sacred tree.

Elizondo-ko batzarra

Zer atsegiña mendian bera
Agertzen gure anaiak
Esanez emen alkartu gera
Izan euskaldun leialak.
Ta ikustean gure artean
Aomen aundiko gizonak
Euskalerriaren sorionean
Argi, maiz egin dutenak.

Elizondo-ko ibar luzean
Egontza eder batean
Amoriozko batasunean
Ikusi ditugu pakean,
Euskaldun onak esku emanik
Jaungoikoaren aurrean
Diotela emen gaude baturik
Lur maitearen onean.

Euskalduna zan Pierre de Marti
Biotz aundiko gizona
Andiskitu nai zuana beti
Jaungoikoaren izena.
Eta gaur ere dator zerutik
Fede bizi bat gugana
Esanez beti, burua zutik
Euskaldun onak gerala.

Town Meeting in Elizondo

It feels good walking
down the mountain
greeting our neighbors,
saying, here we are,
like old time Basques—
even the famous
among us who work
for the nation's good.

In the long and lovely
Elizondo Valley, we see
the Basques, a people
made greater by love,
at peace, shaking hands
before God, brought
here by love of land,
by the land's love.

Pierre de Marti—
Basque, big-hearted,
who glorified God.
Now as then, our
living faith, a voice
from Heaven telling us
that heads held high,
we're worthy Basques.

Oroi gaitezen Santxo Portitzak
Eta Matxin de Mungiak
Zuten bezala izan biotzez
Onratu Euskalerria;
Eta kondairak esan dezala
Mundu dan arte egia
Urez ta lurrez maitatua da
Euskeldun odol garbia.

Izan Elkano ilezkorraren
Fede santu bat bizia
Erregu beti, betor Jaunaren
Zeruetako grazia;
Bera lenengo emen lurrean
Eman ziguna argia!
Bai euskaldunak, Elkanok zuan
Arritu mundu guztia.

Euskalduna zan Peñaflorida
Munibe lenargitia
Ikaz dezagun berak bezela
Onatzen Euskalerria;
Bera lenego elkargoaren
Ipinle argi zuzena
Gaur euskaldunak bear da emen
Onratu bere izena.

Bere jakintza on bidezkoak
Españan ziran zabaldu
Peñaflorida bezelakoak
Gutxi dirade azaldu;
Baina gaur ere uskal leialak
Batu gaitezen alkartu
Eta Munibek zuan bezela
Euskalerria maitatu.

Let's remember Santxo
Portitza[32] and Martin Mungia,[33]
and honor Euskal Herria,
that history may say
of the native Basques
how well loved
they were on land
and at sea.

Be as Elkano,[34]
of immortal living
faith, whose prayer
gained Heaven's grace—
first among us to bring
the light. Yes, it's true,
my dear fellow Basques,
Elkano surprised the world.

Munibe[35]—Basque—
Count of Peñaflorida.
Let's learn as he did
to better Euskal Herria.
He was the one who
turned on the light.
Today we should
honor his name.

His knowledge and deep
thought spread across
Spain. Granted, few
are like Peñaflorida.
Still, faithful Basques
can come together
and as Munibe did,
love Euskal Herria.

Lurreratuak lege zar onak.
Ezbearrean galduak!
Makur gerade gaur euskaldunak.
Erruki gaitu munduak!
Baña gaur ere gizon biotzdunak
Euskaldun garbi prestuak
Beti dituzte gauzik maiteenak
Jaungoikoa eta Fueroak.

The ancient laws are
dead and gone, lost
to misfortune and we
Basques, on our knees,
are pitied. But even today,
honest Basques of good
heart love, above all,
God, those ancient laws.

Ezkongaietan

Ezkongaietan zerbait banintzan,
Ezkondu eta ezer ez;
Ederzalea banintzan ere
Aspertu nintzan ederrez:
Nere gustua egin nuen ta
Orain bizi naiz dolorez.

Nere andrea andre ederra zan
Ezkondu nintzan orduan
Mudatuko zan esperantzakin
Ere, batere ez nuan;
Surik batere baldin badago
Maiz dago aren onduan.

Zokoak zikin, tximak jario,
Aurra zintzilik besoan;
Adabakia desegokia
Gona zarraren zuloan;
Iru txikiko botila aundia
Dauka berakin alboan.

Nere andrea alperra dago,
Ez da munduan bakarrik;
Gauza gozoen zalea da ta
Ez du egin nai bearrik;
Sekulan ere ez da ondo izango
Alakoaren senarrik.

Single

Single, I was something.
Married, I'm nothing.
Chasing after beauty
I grew bored with beauty.
I did what pleased me.
Now I'm wretched.

When I married her,
my wife was a beauty.
I never wanted
that to change.
If the stove's lit,
that's where she sits.

Dirt everywhere, hair
tangled, kid hanging
from her arm, crooked
patch over the hole
in an old skirt. Three
bottles of wine at hand.

My wife's useless.
She's not the only one—
lover of what's easy,
won't do what needs
to be done. With this,
a husband is doomed.

Larunbatetik larunbatera
Garbitzen ditu zatar bi,
Bere aietxek berotutzeko
Erretzen egur zama bi;
Belaun bietan bana artuta
Ez da ixiltzen kantari.

Nere andrea goiz jeikitzen da
Festara bear denean;
Buruko mina egiten zaio
Asi baino len lanean.
Zurekin zer gertatu bear zen
Nik bildurrikan ez nuan.

Saturday to Saturday,
she launders two rags,
burns two loads of wood
to warm her own bum.
Sitting cross legged
she never stops singing.

A holiday—she's up
early. But workdays—
she's got a headache
before she starts.
With you, I lost my fear
of what had to come.

Beltzerena

Beltzerena naizela
Kalean diote,
Ez naiz zuri ederra,
Arrazoia dute;
Eder zuri galantak
Pausuan amabi,
Beltzerenak graziosak
Milaetatik bi.

Beltzerena naizela
Zuk neri esateko,
Lenago zan denbora
Erreparatzeko;
Beltzak eta zuriak
Mendian ardiak;
Zuk ere ez dituzu
Bentaja guztiak.

Beltzerena graziosa
Parerik gabea,
Mundu guztiak dio
Zerala nerea;
Munduak jakin eta
Zuk ez jakitea,
Ondo egiten dezu
Disimulatzea.

Black

The street gossips say
I'm black, not a lovely
white. They're right.
White beauty queens?
A dozen at every step.
Black women who've
got a way with words?
Two in a thousand.

As to me being
black, it took you
a while to notice.
She's black! Black
and white sheep
on the mountain.
You can't have
everything.

Incomparable
black beauty—
everyone says
you're mine.
You do a good
job pretending
not to know what
the world knows.

Sarritan amodioz
Dizut begiratzen,
Arreta guztiakin
Errespetatutzen;
Begiak beltzez beltzak
Itz ori donoso...
Ez det mutilik bear
Orren amoroso.

Again and again,
I look at you—really
look, bow lovingly
before you, eyes
blacker than black,
your way with words.
Such love is not
for little boys.

Euskalerria eta Amerika

Gure Euskalerritik
Ameriketara
Zenbait euskaldun gazte
Pozez joaten dira
Gurasoak utzita
Ondasunen bila,
Esanaz: ama, laister
Etorriko gera.

Egin ama tristeak
Damuzko negarra,
Ontziak onuzkero
Pasa zuen barra;
Izkutatzen danean
Agiri ez dala,
Zeinek daki ai! zer dan
Ama baten pena.

Ez pentsatu an danak
Aberats dirala;
Pobreak ni bezela
Milaka badira;
Ara dijoazenak
Ondasunen bila
Gutxi itzultzen dira
Beren sorterrira.

Euskalerria and America

How many young
Basques, seeking
their fortune, happily
take off for America,
leaving their parents
behind, saying,
"Mother, we'll
be back soon."

And the sorrow
the mothers feel?
The ship has sailed.
Out of sight,
tears of regret
won't bring it back.
No one knows
a mother's grief.

Don't think
it's all easy money
over there, everyone
rich. Thousands,
like me, are broke.
Of those who go
in search of wealth,
few ever come home.

Egia, emen ere
Joan dan aspaldian
Gauza onik ez degu
Euskalerrian;
Oraindaino bezela
Bagabiltza auzian
Emen biziko gera
Beti miserian.

Nere adiskideak,
Bear da pentsatu:
Lujuak miseria
Guztiz gertuan du.
Asi, bada, gaur bertan,
Gona oiek moztu...
Familian pakea
Izango badegu.

Neskatzak diote: goazen
Ameriketara;
An guztiz apainduak
Ibiliko gera...
Bada, gaixoak, joan zan
Jaujaren denbora,
An ere lan eginda
Bizi bearko da.

Eman, adiskideak,
Munduari buelta;
An baino lur oberik
Inun ere ez da;
Eta zerutxoren bat bilatu nai bada,
Emen bertan ditugu
Donosti eta Deba.

I admit it's true
that in Euskal Herria,
too, the good old days
weren't so good.
And if we go on
arguing as we do,
it'll be misery
forever.

Look, friends, think
about it—wealth
sits happily
on poverty's lap.
If we want peace
in the family, we'll
tighten our belts.[36]
Starting today.

The young girls say,
"Let's go to America,
we'll wear fancy
dresses and jewels."
Oh, my poor dears,
the days of the idle
rich are gone. There,
too, you work to live.

Go ahead, friends,
spin the globe—
nowhere better
than where you are.
If you're looking for Heaven,
it's right here—in
Deba and Donosti.[37]

Zuk, ere badakizu
Bai Isabelita
Euskalerria dala
Guztizko polita.
Emen asia zera
Emen zure aita
Lur au berak bezela
Bear dezu maita.

Come on, Isabel,
you know Euskal
Herria is beautiful
beyond compare.
You were born here,
your father before
you. He loved it.
Couldn't you?

Ez bedi galdu euskera

Gure euskera eder maitea
Galtzen gaur degu ikusten,
Euskaldun onak arritzeko da
Nola ez diran lotsatzen!
Larramendirik, Astarloarik
Ez da geiago aipatzen...
Ez da utsegin aundiagorik
Ondo badegu pentsatzen.

Galdu dirade oitura onak,
Galdua dugu Euskera...
Ola bagaude, eun une barru
Galdu da gure izena!
Erro, Aizkibel ziran bezela
Erakusterik gaur ez da.
Gure euskera ...ai! galtzen bada
Gu... euskaldunak ez gera!

Nola isildu eta barkatu?
Etorkizunen kondairak
Arrazoiakin esango digu:
Nun dira zuen oiturak?
Damu dute bai... gaur uskaldunak
Lotsa pixka bat dutenak,
Aspaldi esan duten bezela
Gizonik jakintsuenak.

Let's Not Lose Euskara

Today we see our
beloved language
disappearing. All
these fine Basques
don't seem to notice.
Of Larramendi,[38] Astarloa,[39]
not a word. You couldn't
dream up greater loss.

We're losing our way,
losing Euskara. Go on
like this and in a hundred
years we'll lose ourselves.
We've got no mentors
like Erro,[40] like Aizkibel.[41]
Hell, if there's no Euskara,
there'll be no Euskaldunak.

Are we to be silent?
Forgive? Historians
will look back and ask,
"Where's what makes
you Basque?" Those
who can feel regret
do. The wise have
said it all before.

Dala Parisen eta Londresen
Jakintsu asko badira;
Euskerazko liburu zarren
Ondoren ibiltzen dira...
Or da Luziano, printze ernaia,
Orain guretar deguna,
Euskerazale bikain-bikaina,
Jakintsuetan aundi dena.

Arren, ez bada galdu euskera,
Nere anaia maiteak!
Galzten badegu... galduak gera
Gu eta gure semeak.
Beti euskeraz itz egin, bada,
Oso zaar eta gazteak
Esan ez dedin denok gerala
Euskaldun biotz gabeak.

In Paris and London,
the many learned hunt
up old Basque books.
Take Prince Luziano—[42]
astute, one of us,
our language's best
of best friends, wise
among the wise.

Dear fellow Basques,
hang on to Euskara,
please. Lose it and we
are lost, our children
lost. Young and old,
speak Euskara, always,
that it not be said
we've lost our soul.

Aloñamendi

Aloña mendi aldamenean,
Guztiz leku agirian,
Oñati eder au ikusten da
Zelaitxo baten erdian.

San Migeletan ango jaietan,
Dantzan ta alaitasunian,
Ai! zer egunak pasa ditugun
Bizkaitarren lagundian.

Bergara ta Markina,
Mondragoi ta Oñati,
Gaztedi eder fina
An bai zan galanki.

Partidu ederrak jokatzen ziran
Egun aietan Oñatin;
Jokalari onak nola ziraten,
Onena zein zan nork jakin?

Batzuek zioten: Or Bizimodu,
Besteak «Biba» Gereta;
Mutil gogor au azkar zebilen
Arrapatzeko pelota.

Merlaet ta Marinela,
Zugarri, Gereta,
Aurrean dabilena
Arrimatzen pareta.

Mount Aloña

Below Mount Aloña
in the middle of a vast
open space lies Oñati.
Beautiful Oñati.

The feast of Saint Michael—
what a time we had
with the Bizkaians
dancing for days.

Bergara and Markina,
Mondragón and Oñati—[43]
so many bright, good
looking young people.

In those days they played
elegant handball[44] in Oñati.
Among so many greats,
who knew who was best?

Some said, "Bizimodu."
Others, "Go Gereta,"
strong and quick
to trap the ball.

Merlaet, Marinela,
Zugarri, then Gereta[45]
who plays up front,
hugging the wall.

Marinela da altu zabal bat,
Guztiz jokalari ona,
Bizimodu da aidosua ta
Atzean ematen du lana.

Merlaet, berriz, galai gazte bat
Segurua ta arina;
Zugarri aurrean, ene mutilak,
Ematen du zer egina.

Bizkaian ta Probintzian,
Pelotari onak,
Oberik ez Españan.
«Gora euskaldunak».

Goierriko jende guztia,
Lekaioka ta saltoka,
Umore onean mendiak bera
Oñatira doa lasterka.

Ai! zer egunak, nere lagunak,
Probintzin dira pasatzen;
Oraindik ere oroitutzean
Bereala naiz poztutzen.

Nere adiskide maiteak,
Diberti geranak,
Naiago nuke balitz
San Miguel egunak.

Gora Oñati eder ta zabal
Ta bere jende atsegina,
Kanpotar danok ongi artzeko
Egin dezute alegina.

Marinela—tall, a little
fat but really good.
Bizimodu in the back
court, in control, easy.

The young heart throb
Merlaet—confident,
speedy. Up front, boys,
Zugarri gets it done.

These players in Bizkaia
and Gipuzkoa, none
better in all of Spain.
Long live the Basques!

The Goierri[46] crowd comes
bounding down the mountain,
shouting like crazy, happy,
racing to Oñati.

God, what a time it was,
those days in Gipuzkoa.
Even now, looking back,
friends, I'm smiling.

All of us lifted
beyond ourselves—real
companions. Oh, to relive
the celebration of Saint Michael.

Long live beautiful
generous Oñati—arms
wide to enfold us all
wherever we're from.

Erri onetan alkatea ere
Da leiala ta txit ona,
Danok batean esan dezagun:
Gora gure alkate jauna.

Agur, gaztedi ederra,
Erri au det maitatzen,
Emendik banoa baina
Biotza det gelditzen.

Mila amorio dedan erritik
Penaturikan joan bear
Nere biotzak egingo luke
Bai orain bertatik negar.

Txikia ta aundi, danori, agur,
Bai ere armenteriak,
Adiskideak Kristoren legez
Danok gerade anaiak.

Nere adiskide maiteak,
Oiek dira egunak,
Aberats ta pobreak
Gaur gera lagunak.

Plaza eder artan ibiliagatik
Dantzan, bai, jende guztia,
Umore ona zan danen artean,
Erri guztia pakean.

Neskatxa ederrak agertzen ziran
Su argien artetian;
Ondoren berriz, galai gazteak
Txoraturikan atzian.

In this town even
the mayor is worthy.
Here's to an honest
official—hurrah!

So long, alluring youth.
I love this place!
I may have to go
but my heart stays.

A thousand loves lost,
wrapped up in suffering.
If I listened to my heart
I'd be crying right now.

Goodbye to all, young
and old, even the arms
dealers, our brothers
and sisters in Christ.

Those were the days,
my friends, for once,
rich and poor
on the same side.

In the town square,
all of us dancing,
the spirit moving
among us, at peace.

The beautiful girls
stepping from the fire.
The young don Juans,
behind them, burning.

Danbolin soiñu ederrean
Dantzan gazte eta zarrak,
Zebiltzen umore onean,
Pozetan goierritarrak.

Erriko jaunak atzera zuan
Ilunabarrean dantza;
Ai! ederra eta ikusgarria
Orduan Oñatiko plaza.

Ezin da obeto egin zituan
Jira-bira dantzaurriak;
Ondoren zetozen apaindurik
Bertako dama guztiak.

Dama artean dana
Modu ta grazia,
Arriturik gelditu
Zan jende guztia.

Every soul in Goierri,
young and old, inside
the beat of the drum,
outside themselves.

Then another party—
the town nobleman's.
Oh, it was a sight—
the square, the night.

Whirling, swirling,
the dancer become
the dance, the local
women dressed to kill.

The women, yes, but
all of it—style, grace.
We stood stunned.
Everything stopped.

Sistema metrikoari

Frantzian dana omen da
Dana inkonstanzia:
Baina asmoarentzat
Badute grazia.
Aurerratik ei dago
Gure auzo erria:
Orain ekarri dute
Sistema berria.

(errezitatua)
Ikusiko zenduke
Zeinek entenditu lukeen
Lenguaje ori?
Eskola Maisu Jaunak
Esan dit lengo egunian,
Libra bat aragi
Edo libra bat legatz,
Erostera bazuazte plazara,
Esango omen da:

Kilometro, Ektometro
Dezimetro, Milimetro.
Litro, Ektro, Setro, Netro;
Ai, au diabrukeria!
Zeinek adi lezake lenguaje ori?
Eta Eskola Maisu Jaunari
Asarratuta esan nion.

Here's to the Metric System

It seems like things
in France are always
up in the air but if you
want something new,
that's the place to go.
Now our inventive
neighbor has brought
us a whole new system.

(spoken)
It's like speaking
in tongues—who can
do it? The other day
our learned schoolmaster
said to me, "Let's say
you go to the market
for a pound of meat
or a pound of hake,
you should say

kilometer, hectometer,
decimeter, millimeter."
Liter, eeter, seeter, neeter.
It's nuts! Who could figure
this out? Are these even
words? Seething, I said
to our learned schoolmaster,

(errezitatua eta abestua)
Kilometro, sistema berria
Entenditu ez lezake;
Diabrukeria oiek
Ez dira sartuko nere buruan;
Eta libra, libra erdi,
Laurden, laurden erdi
Esan bearko antxinako moduan,
Ai, onen biziak!

(spoken and sung)
"No one gets this new
kilometer business. It's
devil work, not going in
my head. Say what we
always have—pound, half
pound, quarter pound,
half a quarter pound. Lord
save us from the learned!"

Alegriko traperari

Neska batek besteari esaten zion,
emakumetxuak ikusi al den kabua?
Ez kaborik eta ez sargentorik ere
jende klase orrekin tratatzen degula
pentsatzen al den, neska, ja jai!
conversación y todo lo que se quiere
zipirri zaparra zer nai baino jende
clase orrekin tratatu gutxi, goazen
berriz neska trapuak biltzera.

Egunez trapu biltzen
Gabean dantzan lertzen
Beti umore onean
Ibiltzen gera
Eta goizean goiz
Kalera irten da
Lo gosoan daudenak
Esnatutzeko.

Atera, atera
Trapuak saltzera
Nik erosten det
Modu onetan:
Ardit albarka
Cuarto alpargata[47]
Ta burni zarra
Txanponian.

To the Alegria Rag Picker

One young woman says to another,
"So, girl, have you seen the corporal?"
And the other, "Jesus, sister, don't
even think about hanging out with
those types, not corporals not sergeants.
'Berriketa eta nahi izaten den dena'
then, like that—wham-bam, thank
you ma'am. Don't have anything
to do with them. Let's get back
to work—there are rags
to be gathered."

Rag picking all day,
dancing all night,
leave our worries
behind, then up
at five, and out
on the street
to wake up those
who sweetly sleep.

Come out, come
out, to sell us
your rags. Here's
how I buy them:
sheepskin moccasins,
bedroom slippers,
a lead slug slipped
into the change.

Pluma lori zatar

Pluma lori zatar bat
Zorrozturik gaizki
Asi zan eskribitzen
Arroturik lazki
Gure arbola iltzeko
Asmoetan noski
Obe dute pakean
Nere ustez utzi.

Arbola aitatzean
Erdeldunen mina
Ez dakit nundik duten
Orrelako grina
Mundu guztian dute
Sustraia egina
Errespetatu beze
Aran erregina.

Berak arbola gabe
Ez badaude ongi
Imitatzen dute
Euskal erriari
Orra dana kontserbatu
Gaitzik ez inori
Eta posible balitz
Gu bezela jarri.

Bad Quill

A quill pen, poorly
cut, edge worn,
began its tired tale,
bitter words to cut
down our tree.
If you ask me,
better to leave
us in peace.

Mention the tree
and Spanish speakers
go to pieces—oh,
the pain. I can't
explain this fear,
roots everywhere.
Even the queen
should bow down.

If they're lost
without a tree,
they can copy
Euskadi. Hanging
onto who you
are won't hurt
anyone. Maybe
be like us.

España guztia
Jakinean bego
Euskaldunok ez gera
Jo ta artzen egongo
Arbol maitagarria
Gogor eta bero
Kontserbatuko degu
Orain eta gero.

All of Spain needs
to know that we
Basques will never
be ground down.
Furiously, implacably,
we will cling to
our beloved tree,[48]
now and forever.

Tolosar ongileari

Viva Tolosa eder
Zeru bat egina,
Probintziaren erdian
Dirudi erregina;
Zu ikustian beti
Det amore mina,
Zeren daukazun jende
Guztiz atsegina.

Ai! zer edertasuna
Zelaitxo batian,
Lore eder bat dirudi
Mendi bitartean;
Ez baitzaitut ikusi
Juan dan iru urtian,
Pozez zoratzen nago
Anaien artian.

Probintzia guztia
Umore onian,
Tolosara etortzen da
San Juan egunean;
Danbolin soinu ederra
Adizu kalian,
Guazen zezenetara
Guztiok batian.

To the Good Folk of Tolosa

Viva lovely Tolosa,[49]
queen of Heaven
in the middle
of Gipuzkoa.
I see your people
so at ease
and feel
a burning love.

Beautiful flower
in a meadow
between mountains.
Three years since
I've seen you—
I'm dizzy, head
spinning, happy
to be among friends.

St John's Day—
all of Gipuzkoa,
in fine fettle,
comes to Tolosa.
The roll of drum
beats fills the streets.
Let's go together
then, to the bulls.

Gure Probintzi ederra
Da pare gabia,
Ondo gordetzen badu
Fueroen legia;
Gure lege zar onak
Gordeko dira aisa,
Esan dezagun danok: bai...
Tolosarren gisa.

How to explain
Gipuzkoa's beauty?
You can't. Keep
the old laws there
and they'll be kept
everywhere. Yes,
let's say it—Tolosa's
way, it's the way.

Burnizko bideari

Asmoerak dirade
Gaur nazioetan
Asma orduko egiten
Diranak benetan:
Zeinek usteko zuen
Juan dan urtean
Ori pasako zala
Gure Probintzian?

Probintziak bakarrik
Bear ez dira aitatu
Bada nazio guztiak
Bear degu alkartu:
Eta pasatua pasa
Gorrotuak aztu
Berdin alkar artzeko
Jaunak egin gaitu.

Begira adiskideak
Or Frantzi aldera?
Mundu guztia doa
Lezioak artzera:
Orain bada nai nuke
Eman aditzera
Zergatik bear degu
Gelditu atzera?

Ode to the Iron Road

In all the nations today
people have big goals—
things no sooner
imagined than done.
A year ago, who
would have believed
such would come
to pass in Gipuzkoa.

Not just the Basque
provinces but all
nations must
come together,
let the past lie,
forget old hatreds,
see each other as one,
as God made us.

Look at France,
friends, where
everyone goes
to school.
I'll just offer my
two cents worth—
why should we
be left in the dust?

Viva gure España
Eta asmoerak,
Zeinen enbidia dute
Gure lur ederrak?
Mendi eta zelaiak
Zeinek ditu onenak,
Ardo, gari, olioz
Beterikan danak?

Ekin deiogun bada
Burdin bideari
Eta oso egin arte
Eraso lanari:
Astindu bat emanaz
Lenbailen lurrari
Eta anditasuna
Gure Españari.

Aditzera degunez
Amar urte barru
Baporea asiko da
Jainkoak nai badu:
Ala digute beintzat
Frantsesak agindu
Asiera eman da eta
Alkarri lagundu.

Bertati asi gaitezen
Jaunari erregutzen
Pakean bizi bitez
Dutenak agintzen:
Ah! geiago ez balitz
Gerrarikan sortzen
Beti ibili gabe
Bata bestea iltzen.

Long live Spain
and big goals!
Surely, we're not
envious, we with
our beautiful lands—
mountains and fields,
the best wines,
wheat, and oil.

Let's build
that Iron Road
and not stop
till we're done,
shake this place
up—as quick
as we can—help
Spain grow.

They say within
ten years it'll be
steam power,
God willing—
or the French—
so let's move,
start helping
each other.

Here and now,
pray to God
that our leaders
embrace peace—
or at least don't
start new wars;
no more killing.
If only.

Txardin berriak

Santa Agedatik Altzolara
Altzolatik Debara,
Atozte, atozte lenbaitlen
Bañu gez gaziak artzera.
Ta ni Aiataik barrena banua
Banua txardinak saltzera.

Fresh Sardines

From Santa Ageda to Altzola,
from Altzola to Deba, everyone,
come out, come out, as fast
as you can to the sulphur
hot springs while I pass
through Aia[50] selling sardines.

Ilargi eder

Zeru altuan ilargi eder
Izartxo bire erdian

Nere maitea ikusten nuen
Dantzara zijoanian.

Ia korrika ez zukeaken
Lagun guzien artean.

Zeru altuan ilargi eder
Izartxo bire erdian

Beautiful Moon

High in the sky the beautiful moon
between distant stars.

I saw my love
dancing there.

Surrounded by friends,
she wouldn't have flown.

High in the sky the beautiful moon
between distant stars.

Egualdi izugarria

Ernio gainetikan
Aitzkorri mendira,
Gaur ikaragarrizko
Tximistak badira!
Nekazariak diote
Egualdi au zer da?
Munduaren akabera
Gaur eldu ote da!!

Ara mendia bera,
Urak nun datozen,
Ala ere gizonak
Ez dira bildurtzen:
Nola biziko geran
Ez dute pentsatzen,
Arto eta gariak
Badira ondatzen!!

Aurra atoz onera
Ama onak dio
Jaunari erregutu
Beti bear zaio;
Munduan gauza gutxi
Guk degu balio...
Pentsa ezazu ongi
Gaur gerala jaio!

Threatening Weather

Today from above
Ernio to Mount Aitzkorri,[51]
tremendous flashes
of lightning.
The farmers wonder
what's happening—
maybe today we'll see
the end of the world.

The water pours
down the slope,
but the men
aren't frightened,
aren't thinking,
how will we get by
if the corn and wheat
are washed away?

"Come here, child,"
a mother says,
"We should pray
to God. Worldly
things—they don't
matter. Think
about it—today
we're born."

Nere begi aurrean
Pasa da tximista,
Aritz bat or egin du
Zati... mila puska!
Atoz ene maitea,
Zu nere biotza
Jaungoikoagana beti
Izan esperantza.

Begira eguzkia
Nun degun ikusten,
Aizeak asi dira
Oraintxe onduten;
Asi bertan ezkerrak
Jaunari ematen,
Ara gure gizonak!
Orra nun datozen.

Ama eta umeak
Etxeko atean,
Zoraturikan daude
Aita ikustean.
Musu eta laztanka
Etxe barrenian,
Zori ona nun dago?
Ortxe... baserrian.

Egon baserritarrak
Soseguz pakean
Eguzki argia da
Ernio alderan;
Eta denbora txarra
Etortzen danean,
Gizonak bear du izan
Kalma biotzean.

Before my eyes
the lightning strikes,
blasting an oak
to a thousand pieces.
Come here, love
of my heart.
Trust always
in God above.

Look, the sun
is coming out
and the wind
has dropped.
The men are
coming home.
Now's the time
to give thanks.

Mother and child
in the doorway,
dizzy with delight,
seeing father step
into the house—
hugs and kisses.
Where is happiness?
There on the farm.

Be at peace,
farmers, stay
calm. Sunlight
falls over Ernio.
When weather
threatens, it's
best to keep
our heads.

Arantza zorrotza

Amorioa bai da
Arantza zorrotza
Zeinak zulatzen duen
Portizki biotza;
Eritu gabetanik
Ez liteke goza
Beragandik sarritan
Jaio oi da poza.

Maitasun geiegia
Artzea inori
Zein gauza gaiztoa dan
Progatzen det ongi:
Atsekabez beterik
Gau ta egun beti
Ezur uts biurtutik
Arkitutzen naiz ni.

A Sharp Thorn

Yes, it's true—
love's a thorn
driven deep
into the heart.
Without the bitter,
there'd be no sweet.
Sharp thorn from
which joy is born.

You want to know
how bad it is? Ask me.
I'm the test case
for loving too much.
Night and day,
thorn after thorn.
I've become
a bag of bones.

Amorez eria

Amorez eri nago
Aspaldi onetan,
Zureatik maitea
Gau ta egun penetan!
Arki nezake poza
Badakit nik zertan
Sendatuko nitzake
Zure besoetan.

Nere maite polita
Zutzaz oroitzean
Odola pil pil dabil
Nere biotzean:
Kanpora irten nairik
Alegin guzian
Min txar hau bearko zait
Sendatu iltzian.

Berotasun gozo bat
Zainetik zainera
Nere gorputz guzian
Maite sentitzen da;
Gustoaren pasioz
Sartzen zait ikara
Itzikan ere ezin
Asmatu dedala.

Lovesick

Lately I've felt
lovesick—for you.
Night and day.
I mean it! But
I could be happy,
you know, get
well, wrapped
in your arms.

When I think
of you, love,
my heart pounds,
blood roaring.
I'd like to drive it
out, this exquisite
pain. But death
is the only cure.

A sweet warmth
runs in my veins,
floods my body—
passion, pleasure.
Trembling, I open
my mouth to speak
but can't think
what to say.

Eduki dezazuke
Ongi sinistua
Zeruak naukala ni
Zuretzat artua.
Ez nazu ikusiko
Inoiz mudatua,
Ala egiten dizut
Gaur juramentua.

Adios nere maitea
Sekulan detiko,
Ezkonduko zerade
Ni natorreneko;
Maiteak erantzun dit
Pena andi batekin
Ez naiz ni ezkonduko
Ez bada zurekin.

Heaven made
me for you.
It's true.
You can trust
me on this.
My word once
given is given
for good.

So long forever,
my dear. Or
let's say I return—
you'll be married.
"No," you tell me,
voice breaking,
"I'll marry no one
but you."

Bilbao eta fueruak, pakearentzat

Biribil-bado zer polita dan
Orain Bilbao deitzona,
Mundu guzian artu du fama
Merezimenduz duana.
Bi aldiz gerra, bonba eta bala
Bilbao ez zan ikara
Naiz eta jakin elgo zirala
Numanziarrak bezela.

(Korua)
Biba gure arbola
Gora-bedi gora
Eta maite ez duena
Ez da Euskalduna

Begoñatik da ikusgarria
Lopez Haroren erria.
Or bai or dago jakinduria
Or Euskaldunen argia.
Orain laurak bat izango gera
Oro beltza eta zuria
Zureganatu laster bear da
Euskalerri guzia.

(Korua)

Bilbao and the Old Laws, for Peace

Biribil-bado—nowadays[52]
we call it Bilbao. Beautiful,
its name known round
the world and rightly so.
Twice at war—the bomb,
the bullet, the people
fearless, knowing, as in
Numancia, they would die.[53]

> (Chorus)
> Long live our tree,
> may it stand tall.
> Who doesn't love it
> isn't Basque at all.

From the Basilica of Begoña,[54]
there's a fine view
of the lands of Lopez Haro,[55]
of Basque light and learning.
Now we four will be one—[56]
Carlist and Liberal. Soon
all the Basque Country
must come to you.

> Long live our tree…

Alkar gaitezen anai maiteak
Alkartzea da indarra
Zuri begira daude Arabar
Gipuzkoa ta Nafarra
Bizi pakean laurak batean
Errespetatu arbola
Arrotasunik batere gabe
Euskaldun zarrak bezela.

(Korua)

O gaztelauak! Arren ez izan
Gorrotorikan gugana
Badakizute gure mendiak
Guztiz pobreak dirala
Baina gu lanak ez gaitu aspertzen
Osasun ona degula
Zorion gera ikusten bada
Loraturikan arbola.

(Korua)

Gure anaiak ez dira oroitzen
Ibero zarrak zer ziran
Gaztelaukin ziran Navas-en
Gonzalorekin Granadan
Galde bai galde Okendo zer zan
Inglaterran ta Holandan
O, Españaren betiko onra!
Nor ez da oroitzen Trafalgar?

(Korua)

Walk together, friends,
that's our strength.
Araba, Gipuzkoa, and
Nafarroa look to you
to live in peace, we
four as one, modest,
respecting the tree,
like Basques of old.

Long live our tree…

Honorable Castilians,
please don't hate us.
Yes, our mountains
are poor but work
won't wear us down.
We're a sturdy bunch
and happy if we see
the tree in bloom.

Long live our tree…

Some of us have forgotten
the ancient Iberians—
with the Castilians at Navas,[57]
with Gonzalo at Granada.[58]
Ask in England and Holland
who Okendo was—Spain's
honor forever. Who doesn't
remember Trafalgar?[59]

Long live our tree…

Ez gerturatu gerra soinuan
Numanzia bigarrenera
Cid-en semeak nai dutenean
Betor anaiak bezela.
Gu beti gora zuzen bidean
O bai! Gernika maitera
Gure arbola beltzez jantzia
Makurturik ikustera.

(Korua)

Ai! bizi balitz aita maitea
Arrieta Maskarua
Eta arbola bedinkatua
Ikusi lurreratua
Esango luke, Zer da Bizkaia
Galdu ezkero fueroak?
Penagarrizko anima eria
Da gaur Bizkaia gaisoa.

(Korua)

Jauna begira zure semeak
Il naian bata bestea
Emen iguzu lengo legeak
Izan dezagun pakea
Gerra dakigu dala infernua
Bada anaien artean
Betor gugana zure erreinua
Arbolarekin batean.

(Korua)

Don't show up with sabers
rattling as if it's Numancia
all over. When El Cid's[60]
children come, let them
come as friends. We're
going to beloved Gernika,
yes, to see our tree, bent
low, dressed in black.

Long live our tree...

Oh, if our dear father
Arrieta Maskarua[61] had
lived to see the blessed
tree fallen, he'd say,
"What is Bizkaia
if the old laws are lost?"
Unfortunate Bizkaia
with its tormented soul.

Long live our tree...

Look, Lord, on your
children, living to kill
one another. Let's bring
back the old laws, live
in peace. We know
war between ourselves
is hell. May our tree
and your reign be one.

Long live our tree...

Arbola Santu amoriozkoa
Nolatan erori zera
Zu, euskaldunen konsuelua
Zori oneko argiera
Baina oraindik piztuko zera
Esperantzatan bai gera
Orduan igo lainuetara
Makurtu gabe lurrera.

(Korua)

Holy tree of love,
consolation and blessed
light of the Basques,
how could you fall?
Even now, you live
in our hopes, unbent,
risen from the earth
into the clouds.

Long live our tree…

Notes

1 The four provinces of the southern Basque Country—
   Gipuzkoa, Bizkaia, Araba, and Nafarroa.

2 "The authorities" are the Basque civil authorities.

3 "They" are the Spanish authorities who, when Iparra-
   girre returned to the Basque Country from exile in 1855,
   imprisoned him because of the intense feelings that his
   songs stirred in the minds of the people.

4 Euskal Herria, Euskadi, and Euskalerria are different
   ways to refer to the Basque Country in Basque.

5 Mr. Romero Jiménez and Mr. Olaso helped Iparragirre
   return to the Basque Country.

6 Joxe Franzisko Aizkibel, born Azkoitia, Gipuzkoa (1798),
   died Toledo, Spain (1864?). It's said that Aizkibel learned
   Latin before Spanish and that in recognition of his up-
   rightness and capability the church sent him to Rome
   where he served as an abbot's secretary. He later trav-
   eled throughout Europe as secretary to a Granadan duke.
   He sought out books written in Basque and translated
   many works from Spanish to Basque. As a lexicogra-
   pher, Aizkibel argued for standardized Basque spelling
   and grammar to facilitate more widespread learning and
   use of the language. He proposed that the Spanish C
   and QU be replaced with Z and K and that the Spanish
   G be uniformly pronounced with the hard G sound as in
   get going. He was the first writer in the southern Basque
   Country to suggest these changes which have become
   standard in contemporary Basque. He is most known
   today for these orthographic reforms and for his Spanish
   to Basque dictionary.

7   Euskaldunak gara means we are Basque. I left this line in Basque to emphasize the point of the poem and hope it's not too hard a stretch for English language readers.

8   Antonio de Oquendo or, in Basque, Andoni de Okendo, 1577-1640, Spanish admiral, commander of the defeated Spanish forces at the 1639 engagement with Dutch forces at the Battle of the Downs. Born in Donostia, he had an upsy-downsy career. Ordered to command Spain's Atlantic navy, he refused and was arrested. His prison term was converted to forced residence in a convent. Released, he was put in command of the transport of silver from the Andes which led to his being charged with fraud and nepotism. Though not convicted, he was barred from commanding in the silver trade for four years. After successfully landing troops to take Pernambuco, Brazil from the Dutch, he was promoted. He was fined 12,000 ducats for losing two of his ships. He was arrested for dueling. Refusing to reinforce the fleet of the Kingdom of Naples, he was punished by being made governor of Mahón, the capital of Menorca. Injured in the Spanish loss at the Battle of the Downs, he returned to A Coruña, Spain where he died. A Spanish war vessel named for Okendo burned and sank during the Spanish American War.

9   Mainazi is the Basque abbreviation for María Ignacia.

10 Billareal de Urretxu is a town in Gipuzkoa on the road from Beasain to Bergara, butted up against Zumarraga. Since 1981 its official name has been Urretxu. It was Iparragirre's birthplace.

11 Lorenzo Latorre, full name Lorenzo Antonio Inocencio Latorre Jampen (1844-1916), was the dictator and president of Uruguay from March 1876 to March 1880. Instrumental in two coups that brought him to power, in 1879, he ran for and was elected president. He abolished the rule that required non-white Uruguayans to serve in the army saying such compulsory service for one segment

of the population betrayed the fundamental principles of equal rights and the "democratic principles to which we adhere." Life is full of contradictions.

12 Txurruka was Cosme Damián de Churruca y Elorza (1761-1805), born in Mutriku, Gipuzkoa—about half-way between Donostia and Bilbao. An Admiral of the Spanish Armada, he is known for his courage, daring, and naval skill in the Battle of Trafalgar when he famously nailed the Spanish flag to the mast of his ship letting the British know he would fight to the end. He did.

13 Don Garcia king of Navarre, well, there were about a million kings of Nafarroa named Garcia but this is Santxo Garces I (860-925 C.E.), ruler from 905 to 925 of what was then known as the kingdom of Pamplona. He was part of the force that defeated Islamic armies in 920 at the battle of Balde-Junkera. Balde-Junkera comes from val de Junquera—the Junkera Valley. No one knows exactly where the site of the battle was.

14 This refers to the four southern Basque provinces.

15 Oral tradition holds that people from Antzuola defeated the Muslims at the battle of Balde-Junkera in 920 C.E.

16 Uzarraga is one of the neighborhoods of Antzuola.

17 Gabiria is a community located ten miles from Antzuola.

18 Fueristas or foruzaleak in Basque – from the word foru, fuero, fors, the ancient laws that governed the Basque Country and its relationship to surrounding kingdoms, peoples, and nations. A fuerista would be likely to support Basque autonomy and in a modern context, political autonomy and the creation of an independent Basque nation state.

19 Here, fellow Iberians refers to the other nations of the Iberian Peninsula—Catalans, Spaniards, Galicians, Andalucians, Asturians, Cantabrians, Aragonese, and everybody else who isn't Basque.

20 Jaun Zuria—the White Gentleman or White Noble-
man—is the mythical first Lord and founder of the Lord-
ship of Bizkaia (1040-1876 C.E.) who defeated Leonese
and Asturian troops in the also mythical Battle of Padura,
driving the enemy to the Malato (sickened) tree and thus
establishing the borders of Bizkaia. Jaun Zuria was the
son of the Basque creator destroyer God Sugaar and a
Scottish princess who happened to be in Mundaka where
she could be impregnated by a God. It's a complicated
story with political implications beyond us here.

21 Nafarroa is one of the seven Basque provinces.

22 Another reference to the four southern Basque prov-
inces.

23 Iruña or Iruñea is the Basque name for the city of Pam-
plona.

24 Black and White – during the Carlist Wars in the nine-
teenth century the Carlist forces were symbolized as the
White and the Liberal forces as the Black.

25 A town in the Baztan Valley in Nafarroa.

26 Here, Iparragirre refers to a Basque nationalist political
assembly held in Elizondo.

27 Mateo Benigno Moraza (1817-1878) was a Basque jurist
and politician who was also an ardent fuerista or foruzale.

28 Basque name for the city of Vitoria.

29 Adriaan Hans Pater (Hauspaster), Dutch naval com-
mander defeated after a six-hour fight on September 12,
1631 by Okendo's forces at the Battle of los Abrojos in
Brazil. Abrojos means caltrops—either the star thistle or
a spiked metal device designed in such a way that a point
always faces upward when placed on the ground—used
to puncture tires or feet or anything needing puncturing.

30 Bezerro Bengoa – this was Ricardo Becerro de Bengoa,
the journalist who reported in the newspaper *La Paz*

on September 16, 1876 that, contrary to rumors in the Basque Country, Iparragirre was alive. Bezerro de Bengoa charged his brother Julián with finding the missing poet and was instrumental in organizing the subscription campaign to pay Iparragirre's passage home and to set up the concert that Iparragirre was to give upon his return.

Daniel Arrese (1831-1891) was a Basque writer, teacher, and journalist. Arrese was one of the founders of the newspaper *El Alavés* and wrote for other newspapers such as *El Porvenir Alavés*, *El Fuerzaista* and *El Ateneo*. Renowned fuerista or foruzale, he was the author of numerous works on Basque culture.

Fermín Herrán (1852-1908) was one of the most prominent Basque authors of Eusko Pizkundea, the Basque cultural renaissance of the nineteenth century. He was the founder of Biblioteca Bascongada and directed the journal *Revista de las Provincias Euskaras*.

Sotero Manteli (1820-1885) was a Basque writer and printer who with other writers founded the magazine *Vascongada* in 1846. Manteli worked for the dissemination of Basque culture and wrote for many publications.

31 Foruak, singular foru – the ancient laws that governed the relations of the Basque communities with each other and with non-Basque peoples and nations. Rulers of principalities and kingdoms that had contact with the Basques came to the meeting place at the tree of Gernika in Bizkaia to swear allegiance to these old laws—the foruak—and to recognize the autonomy of the Basque Country, to assure the Basque people that their language and practices would be forever respected. Over the centuries of Spanish and French rule the scope of the foruak grew ever narrower. The emperor Napoleon accelerated the erosion of the foruak in France. The Carlist wars in nineteenth century Spain brought increasing pressure on the foruak. Finally, with the end of the Spanish civil war in 1939 and the beginning of fascist rule in Spain under

Francisco Franco, the last of the foruak were abolished by the Spanish state though since the death of Franco in 1975, the Basque people have regained some of their historic rights.

32 Santxo Bortitza or Sancho VII the Strong (1154-1234 C.E.) was a king of Nafarroa.

33 Martin or Matxin Mungia was a Basque soldier who fought under Andrea Doria against the Turks in the battle of Previsa in 1538. He also fought in the defense of Castelnuovo in 1539 where he was taken prisoner by Hayreddin Barbarossa. Barbarossa gave Mungia the choice of converting to Islam and serving Ottoman Monarch Suleiman the Magnificent or being killed. Mungia chose death and was executed on the spur of Barbarossa's galley.

34 Juan Sebastián Elcano (1476-1526), born in Getaria, Gipuzkoa, Elcano was a member of Ferdinand Magellan's 1519-1522 expedition to circumnavigate the globe. After Magellan's death in the Philippines, then the death of two further commanders, Elcano was selected by the expedition's surviving sailors to serve as captain and complete the voyage which he did and so became the first person we know of to sail around the world. In words reminiscent of Bertolt Brecht's in his poem "A Worker Reads and Asks These Questions," Elcano sailed around the world. Did no one sail with him?

35 Xabier Mari de Munibe e Idiáquez, Count of Peñaflorida, founded the Royal Basque Society of Friends of the Country in Bergara in 1748. It became the first economic society of Friends of the Country and was linked to the Real Compañía Gipuzkoana de Caracas. The Friends of the Country were a discussion and debating society promoting enlightenment values. They also sponsored musical and literary performances. Munibe wrote two Basque Spanish bilingual comic operas.

36 Tighten our belts seemed an apt metaphor for the Basque saying gona oiek moztu which literally means shorten those skirts but is used to say we need to economize. If you shorten the skirts, you buy less cloth and so save money.

37 Deba and Donosti are two coastal Basque cities in Gipuzkoa.

38 Manuel Larramendi (1690-1766) was a Jesuit priest and professor. He wrote the first Basque grammar *El imposible vencido: arte de la lengua vascongada* which might be translated as *Overcoming the Impossible: The Art of the Basque Language*. He strove to counteract the view held in his time that Basque was a primitive language lacking in nuance and incapable of expressing the fullness of human experience. He also wrote a Basque Spanish Latin dictionary to show that Basque had a developed vocabulary. He invented many words using Basque roots and grammatical structures while avoiding Latin words even those of non-Latin origin.

39 Pablo Pedro de Astarloa y Agirre (1752-1806) was a Basque priest and linguist who proposed that Basque was the first human language. According to Astarloa, Basque was the perfect language—spoken in the Garden of Eden.

40 Juan Bautista Erro (1773-1854) was a Basque archaeologist, politician, and linguist. He continued the works of Pablo Pedro Astarloa and Juan Antonio Zamacola and in his book *The Primitive Language of Spain* he advocated for the phylogenetic relationship between the Basque and Iberian languages.

41 Joxe Franzisko Aizkibel (1798-1864?) – the same Aizkibel mentioned in the poem "Gora euskera" / "Wagging the Basque Tongue."

42 Prince Louis Lucien Bonaparte (1813-1891) was the third son of Napoleon Bonaparte's brother Lucien. Born in

Worcestershire, England where his father had been interned after being captured by the British while fleeing Italy for the United States, Louis Lucien later served in the French national legislature as a representative of Corsica. A philologist, Louis Lucien's work was instrumental in France's 1883 Linguistic Charter for the Basques. His classification of the Basque dialects is still in use.

43 Bergara, Markina, Mondragón (Arrasate), and Oñati are four Basque cities.

44 Basque handball or esku pilota is one of the most celebrated Basque national sports.

45 Bizimodu, Gereta, Merlaet, Marinela, and Zugarri are the names of handball players of the day.

46 Goierri (the Basque Highlands) is a valley in Gipuzkoa.

47 Abarkak are the most traditional style of footwear in the Basque country. They are made from a single piece of leather laced up around the sock to just below the knee. Abarkak were largely replaced by espadrilles called alpargata in Spanish and Basque. Both shoe styles have been in use for thousands of years and both are associated in the Basque region with country people. The more Basque word for alpargata is espartin derived from esparto, a perennial grass woven to make cords, baskets, and the soles of canvas or cotton topped shoes. English has the word rope-soled sandals and that's kind of an espadrille though in English espadrille often implies dance shoes. In the poem the shoe is a cuarto alpargata, literally a room espadrille which in terms of contemporary American usage I thought might best be rendered as house slipper or bedroom slipper. Maybe I should have said espadrille as that word wants to be remembered in light of the ragpicker going out dancing at night. You can see how hopeless the life of a translator can be. Still, not nearly as hopeless as that of a nineteenth century Basque ragpicker.

48 The tree of Gernika.

49 Tolosa is a Basque town in Gipuzkoa.

50 Santa Ageda, Altzola, Deba, and Aia are towns in the Basque Country.

51 Ernio and Aitzkorri (or Aizkorri) are mountains in Gipuzkoa.

52 Biribil-bado – Here, Iparragirre uses an old name for Bilbo. Some suggest that Bilbao is derived from the combination of the Basque words for river and cove: Bil-Ibaia-Bao. The historian José Tussel Gómez believed that Bilbao is a natural evolution of the Spanish words bello—beautiful—and vado, a shallow spot in a river where one can cross on foot or horseback. The journalist Esteban Calle Iturrino believed that Bilbo's name was derived from the names of the two settlements that existed on the banks of the estuary—Billa and Vaho. Given the similar pronunciation of the Spanish V and B, that's possible. Still, Iparragirre uses Biribil-bado. Biribil is a Basque word meaning spherical or perfect while vado may be that shallow spot in the river where one can cross.

53 Numancia (also Numantia) was a Celtiberian town along the Duero River south of the current Basque Autonomous Community. It's known for its heroic defense against the armies of imperial Rome which invaded in 157 B.C.E. After over twenty years of battles, the Roman senate ordered Numancia destroyed, sending 30,000 troops to attack a population that was thought to be between four and eight thousand. Preparing for an extended siege, the Roman troops built a nine-kilometer fence around Numancia along with towers, moats, and impaling rods. Resistance was hopeless but the people of Numancia refused to surrender to Rome. After eight months during which famine killed much of the population, Numancia's surviving citizens chose to commit suicide rather than become Roman slaves. A few hundred of the inhabitants who had chosen not to kill themselves

surrendered to the Romans but before doing so they burned Numancia to the ground. In Spanish the phrase defensa numantina is used to indicate a desperate suicidal last ditch stand against overwhelming odds.

54 The Basilica of Our Lady of Begoña is a church in Bilbao built on the site where the Virgin Mary is said to have appeared at the beginning of the sixteenth century C.E. Construction began in 1519.

55 Diego López de Haro (circa 1250-1310 C.E.) - founder of Bilbao, son of Diego López de Haro (the third) and grandson of Diego López de Haro (the second). All three were Lords of Bizkaia and sometimes of Araba. You'd think these families could come up with other names although because Iparragirre gives only López de Haro in his poem, we may be forgiven for also remembering Méncia (or Mécia) López de Haro (circa 1215-1270 C.E.), who was born in Bizkaia the daughter of the second López de Haro. When her first husband Álvaro Pérez de Castro, through mismanagement and military adventuring managed to create a famine in his fiefdom and so was forced to go to the king of Castille for aid, the Islamic ruler of Arjona invaded the largely unprotected town of Martos where Méncia had been left on her own. Dressed as a soldier she walked up and down the parapets in full view. The invading forces, thinking there were only women defenders held back, giving the Christian troops time to return. Stunned by his wife's courage and clever action, Álvaro hurried home but fell ill and died. Remarried, Méncia is often remembered as the unpopular Queen of Portugal who her detractors say bewitched her husband, a fine and noble king until his marriage and subsequent ruin. Why is it that we hear this story so often—the fine and noble (male) king who is ruined by his bad wife?

56 The four as one expresses the hope of unity for the four southern Basque provinces.

57 This refers to the battle of Las Navas de Tolosa, said to have been fought on July 16, 1212 C.E.

58 Gonzalo Fernández de Córdoba y Enríquez de Aguilar (1453 – 1515) was a Spanish general and statesman who commanded successful military campaigns leading to the surrender of Granada. Known as El Gran Capitán, Gonzalo was named duke of this and that by Ferdinand II of Aragon—duke of Terranova, of Santángelo, of Andria, of Sessa, of Montalto, also viceroy of Naples. Gonzalo was the first to introduce gunpowder firearms into battle and some call him the father of trench warfare. There you have it.

59 Trafalgar is the battle in which Basque born Admiral Txurruka famously nailed the Spanish flag to the mast of his ship to let the British know he would fight to the death.

60 Rodrigo Díaz de Vivar (1048-1099 C.E.), known as Cid Campeador, was a Castilian nobleman, legendary mercenary, and warrior.

61 Joxe Mikel de Arrieta eta Mascarua Sarachaga (1771-1869) was a Carlist and reform oriented Catholic who lived by the motto Jaungoikoa eta foruak—God and the Old Laws.

62 The materials listed here include the biographical information on Iparragirre's life that is mentioned in the foreword to this book.

Bibliography[62]

Amuriza, Xabier, "Iparragirre bertsolari", Jakin, No. 19-20, 1981, pp. 149-158.

Arana Martija, Jose A., "Iparraguirre y el folklore vasco", Jentilbaratz: Cuadernos de Folklore, No. 1, 1983, pp. 121-128.

Arana, Ander et al., *Iparragirre*, Euskaltzaindia, Bilbao, 1987.

Aulestia, Gorka, "Euskal Literatura Ameriketan (1876-1914)", Sancho el Sabio: Revista de cultura e investigación vasca = euskal kultura eta ikerketa aldizkaria, No. 29, 2008, pp. 65-86.

Belaustegui, Jon J., *Iparragirreren olerki-eresien bilduma ta eritzi laburra*, [s.n.], [s.l.], 1985.

Calleja, Seve, *Iparragirreren gitarra Ameriketan = La guitarra de Iparraguirre en América*, Bizkaiko Foru Aldundia, Bilbao, 2019.

Castresana, Luis de, *Iparragirre'ren bizitza*, La Gran Enciclopedia Vasca, Bilbao, 1978.

------------, *Vida y obra de Iparraguirre: seguida de la obra completa*, La Gran Enciclopedia Vasca, Bilbao, 1971.

Contamine de Latour, Emmanuel, *Guernikako-arbola, chant patriotique basque*, [s.n.], Bagnères-de-Bigorre, 1898.

Fagoaga, Isidoro, "Jose Maria Iparragirre", Egan: Euskalerriaren Adiskideen Elkarteko Boletinaren Euskarazko Gehigarria, No. 1-6, 1976, pp. 71-92.

Gabiria, Julen, *Jose Mari Iparragirre*, Elkarlanean L.G., Donostia, 2001.

Iparragirreri omenaldia bere mendeurrenean 1820-1881: Iparraguirre Erakusketa: bere musika eta kultur ingurua abuztuaren 17tik-31ra = Homenaje a Iparraguirre en su centenario 1820-1881: Exposición de Iparraguirre: Su entorno musical y cultural: del 17 al 31 de agosto de 1981, Museo San Telmo, Donostia, XLII Quincena Musical, Caja de Ahorros Municipal, Donostia, 1981.

Iriondo, Luis, *Iparragirre: Zure oroiz. Piano taxuketat = adaptaciones al piano*, Canciones del Mundo D. L., Madrid, 1983.

Jaka Legorburu, Jaka; Cruz, Ángel, *Iparragirre en el centenario de su muerte = bere heriotzaren mendeurrenean*, Argitalpen eta Publikapenen Gipuzkoar Erakundea, Donostia, 1982.

Lekuona, Juan Mari, "Iparragirre eta bertsolaritza", *Ahozko euskal literatura*, Erein, Donostia, 1982, pp. 189-209.

Lekuona, Juan Mari, *Ahozko euskal literatura*, Erein, Donostia, 1982.

Linazasoro, Iñaki, *Jose Maria Iparraguirre*, Ediciones de la Caja de Ahorros Provincial de Guipuzcoa, Donostia, 1977.

Mendibil, Gontzal, *Iparragirre : erro-urratsak = raíz y viento*, Keinu, Igorre, 1999.

Mitxelena, Koldo, *Historia de la literatura vasca*, Erein, Donostia, 1988.

San Martin, Juan, "Iparragirreren damua", Egan: Euskalerriaren Adiskideen Elkarteko Boletinaren Euskarazko Gehigarria, No. 1-2, 1997, pp. 218-219.

Made in the USA
Middletown, DE
17 March 2021